I0796820

About Island Press

Since 1984, the nonprofit organization Island Press has been stimulating, shaping, and communicating ideas that are essential for solving environmental problems worldwide. With more than 1,000 titles in print and some 30 new releases each year, we are the nation's leading publisher on environmental issues. We identify innovative thinkers and emerging trends in the environmental field. We work with world-renowned experts and authors to develop cross-disciplinary solutions to environmental challenges.

Island Press designs and executes educational campaigns, in conjunction with our authors, to communicate their critical messages in print, in person, and online using the latest technologies, innovative programs, and the media. Our goal is to reach targeted audiences—scientists, policy makers, environmental advocates, urban planners, the media, and concerned citizens—with information that can be used to create the framework for long-term ecological health and human well-being.

Island Press gratefully acknowledges major support from The Bobolink Foundation, The Curtis and Edith Munson Foundation, The Forrest C. and Frances H. Lattner Foundation, The Freedom Together Foundation, The Kresge Foundation, The Summit Charitable Foundation, Inc., and many other generous organizations and individuals.

If You Want to Win, You've Got to Fight

If You Want to Win, You've Got to Fight

A GUIDE TO EFFECTIVE TRANSPORTATION ADVOCACY

Carter Lavin

ISLANDPRESS | Washington | Covelo

Library of Congress Control Number: 2025935891

All Island Press books are printed on environmentally responsible materials.

Manufactured in the United States of America
10 9 8 7 6 5 4 3 2 1

Keywords: bicycle advocacy; bike bus; bike lanes; bike train; budget fight; bus lanes; bus rapid transit (BRT); campaigning; candidate questionnaire; climate activism; coalition building; department of transportation; disruptive action; high-speed rail; highway removal; inside game; inside/outside game; ladder of engagement; Metropolitan Planning Organization (MPO); outside game; pedestrian infrastructure; petitioning; policy fight; political activism; political organizing; political tactics; power map; protected bike lane; public transportation; speed bump; status quo; street safety; traffic calming; traffic violence; transit; transit agency; transportation; transportation activism; transportation advocacy

This book is dedicated to you, reader.
Thank you for wanting to make the world a better place.
I hope this book helps you along your journey.

Contents

Introduction

A protected bike lane that goes to your favorite park, a speed bump that protects your family, a high-speed rail network that connects you with friends, or a bench at your bus stop that lets you rest while you wait: Countless changes like these are possible, and this book will teach you how to win them.

Nearly every day, I work at the boundary between the status quo and the imaginary, bringing transportation possibilities into reality. When it's easy, it's just "bringing." Other times, it's building, coaxing, easing, cultivating, or dragging. I am not particularly special, but I am experienced. I've helped win new bike racks in the fare-gated area of my local Bay Area Rapid Transit (BART) station, a halt on a proposed 20 percent bus fare increase, $3 million for new street safety infrastructure in my city, and $1 billion for California transit systems. This book will teach you lessons I've learned as an activist who has waged hundreds of campaigns at the local, state, and federal levels and advised over seven hundred transportation advocates in rural communities, small towns, suburbs, big cities, red states, and blue states. It also contains wisdom from interviews with dozens of transit, bike, and street safety advocates. With this knowledge, you can make your dreams real.

This book will not tell you what to want; I assume you already have some dreams. You might want cargo bike storage at your local grocery store, or a pedestrian plaza in your downtown that would be the envy of any European city. Maybe you want a protected bike lane network throughout your community to rival the Netherlands, a bus rapid transit system that's better than Bogotá's, or a high-speed rail line that makes the international community say, "Why can't we be like those Americans?" You may have a vision for transportation change that comes from personally experiencing a problem that needs fixing. Or you might not yet have a firm goal in mind and instead want things to be different in general. Maybe you draw inspiration from videos, books, social media posts, or articles that show you how much better the world could be.

Whatever it is you want, I want you to have it. Winning your transportation dream normalizes it, which makes it easier for all of us to win the transportation dreams we are fighting for. And frankly, when it comes to improving our public transportation systems, if you win it, then we all get to use it. If you dedicate your life to getting a high-speed rail network built connecting cities across America and you win, then everyone else can hop on that train too. As the saying goes, our liberation is bound up together.

Our individual efforts also set the stage for huge collective wins. Winning something truly transformational, like hundreds of billions in annual federal funding for transit, takes advocates like you and me organizing in every corner of the country pushing our representatives in that direction. Advocates do not have to intentionally collaborate, though that helps, but as long as we are pushing in the same direction, we can win big together.

Achieving Your Transportation Dream Means Getting Political

Winning these changes means getting political. Politics is "the total complex of relations between people living in society," and almost nothing is as political as how people get around.[1] Society affects where we go and how we go, and in turn, how we transport ourselves affects society. When a person is on roads, sidewalks, waterways, rails, or in the sky, they are taking up space and using infrastructure that has been planned, designed, financed, and built by others. When you try to change anything about those spaces, like adding a sidewalk or a protected bike lane, you are doing work that is political.

If someone tries to stop you and keep things the way they are, that's also political. In the American transportation system, business as usual—also called the status quo—means prioritizing cars over people. However, our system is not inherently or inevitably pro-car and anti-people. This status quo was made and is maintained by political decisions. Our transportation systems would literally crumble without consistent maintenance, as Alan Weisman describes in his book *The World Without Us*. For a mundane example of this, check out your local pothole.

Each time a government sets its budget is an opportunity to direct its spending in a way that either affirms or reimagines the car-centric status quo. It is an active choice for local, state, and federal governments to spend roughly $200 billion on highways and roads each year.[2] Beyond these financial costs, our systems designed around cars also cost us our health and our planet. Maintaining the status quo is a political choice.

By consistently choosing to prioritize cars over people, our elected officials have left millions of Americans with no viable option besides cars. Among US adults, 47 percent want to ride bikes more often than they do but are afraid of getting hit by cars.[3] Half of Americans do not have access to public transportation.[4] In transit discussions, people talk about two types of riders: "choice riders," who take transit because they choose to, and "captive riders," who take transit because driving isn't an option for them—like the third of Americans who are unable to drive.[5] While many car drivers are "choice" drivers, millions are "captive" drivers because they don't have other choices. Everyone deserves better mobility options.

Transportation politics are so inherent to our everyday lives that there is no neutral ground: Transportation choices either challenge our status quo or they support it. It's easy to identify something as "political" when it challenges the status quo, but upholding the transportation status quo is also political because it impacts others. For example, a choice as innocent as driving to run an errand is still political regardless of intention, because it affects others by adding to congestion and pollution. A person can challenge the status quo by choosing to bike instead, and they can challenge it even more by choosing to tell politicians to build a protected bike lane network.

Transportation activists can help give people more choices in how they get around and create opportunities for them to get involved in reshaping their community. When you seek to get others to join you in "being political," that's called "politically mobilizing" and "politically organizing." Most of this book focuses on how to intentionally engage politically to win what you want by collectively fighting for it and collaborating with others who share your dream. Chapter 1 builds on the foundational point that transportation is always political. Every transportation change is a political matter and is almost always a political fight. You cannot get billions of dollars in high-speed rail funding, block an airport expansion, get a new bus route, protect a bike lane, or win a speed bump by only asking nicely.

Like most political issues, transportation generates intense debate because people tend to have opinions about how the world works and how it should work. They have really strong opinions about perceived threats to the things they consider theirs. "That bike lane will destroy my parking" is a standard objection to almost every bike project. To be fair, they are partially right—that parking spot is theirs and that street is theirs too. But one person is not the sole owner of a public street parking spot. "Their" parking spot and "their" street also belong to you, me, and everyone else. Street safety and transit are public goods that benefit us all, but there is always opposition from people who believe that those changes mean they lose "their" thing, whether that is "their" parking space, "their" road space, or a perception of ownership of "their" community.

Transportation changes can ignite a political firestorm. American communities consistently fight over relatively minor proposed changes to the transportation status quo. Even in a climate-conscious California city like Berkeley, a bike lane proposal turned neighbors on each other as part of a "culture war."[6] It's not just bikes: All forms of transportation are a tinderbox of controversy. Florida and Indiana legislatures have even gone so far as to consider policies to ban bus-only lanes. Even something as small and reasonable as a speed bump is political and can incite rabid opposition from neighbors who don't like change.

It might seem a bit melodramatic, but that's America today. Unless transportation advocates internalize that truth, we will consistently end up bringing a knife to a gunfight. To be extremely clear: Transportation advocates should not shy away from these fights. You can win in spite of that pushback by out-organizing your opposition and pushing harder. This book will teach you how. But you cannot win change if you refuse to engage in the political fight for it.

Some readers might struggle with accepting the idea that these are political fights; chapter 1 is especially for them. Parts of the transportation advocacy community have a strong tendency to think that if only they could propose the perfect policy or the perfect message, then there would be no opposition. But you can present a great idea to a decision-maker and have all the facts on your side and still be met with, "So what?" Advocate Anna Zivarts, author of *When Driving Is Not an Option: Steering Away from Car Dependency*, said in our interview, "So many people want to know, 'What is the thing that I need to do to fix this? What is the right policy solution?'" But, she says, "I don't actually think that's the problem. . . . That's not really what's stopping us from moving forward. It is a political question."[7] For example, the policy question of how we get more people on transit has many straightforward solutions like opening all the fare gates and getting rid of all fare boxes on buses to make transit free. However, the political matter of actually getting a transit agency to do that is a lot harder than coming up with the policy solution.

It can be tempting to view transportation issues as logic problems rather than political struggles. Figuring out the most efficient way for lots of people to get around a community is in fact a geometry problem, and it has a logical solution: Prioritize walking, rolling, biking, scooters, and transit. But politics is a power struggle. While transportation advocates may be right, we often lose because we are not politically strong enough to get the decision-makers to back our solutions. Time and again, transportation advocates' experiences have affirmed that being right is one thing and winning is another. Laura Chu Wiens, the executive director of Pittsburghers for Public Transit, explained that when it comes to winning, "It doesn't matter if you're right. It never matters if you're right. . . . You just have to have the power to win the thing. . . . Beyond helping motivate our side, being right has never helped us win anything."[8]

Winning by Building Political Power

Once we accept the truth that transportation is always political and winning the fight for change takes power, then we can be more strategic in our advocacy. Accepting this truth can help us move beyond asking why our communities don't have the transportation features other places have. Now we have the answer: Nobody who has wanted it, including you, has used enough political power to make it happen. No one fought for it effectively enough before now. That is a painful truth, but it frees us up to consider a more productive question: How can I build political power with others and use that to win what we want?

I wrote this book to help answer that question for you. Winning takes a lot of work, but it is doable. Sometimes it's a wonderful way to build joyous community and befriend people you otherwise wouldn't have. Sometimes it's frustrating and heartbreaking. Sometimes you do the best you can and still lose, and sometimes you stumble into surprisingly easy wins. This book will help you through those highs and lows.

When you know how to do it well, building political power can be easy. It is not that hard to get a person waiting for a bus to sign a petition demanding politicians provide more funding for transit. That is a straightforward conversation to have, but you need to have it over and over again with a lot of different people. The legendary farmworker organizer César Chávez once said that politically organizing is simple: "First you talk to one person, then you talk to another person, then you talk to another person."[9]

This work of building connections and community can feel empowering, and it can be exhilarating to see your victory become more possible. In fact, it can become so enticing that your activism will often snowball into more activism. Win a protected bike lane once and you might be very tempted to try and win another one. I am a bit addicted to politically organizing, or in other words, bringing more people into transportation activism. I try to limit myself to pursuing "only" about half a dozen campaigns during any given week.

While working on this book I also codeveloped a board game about political organizing and trained hundreds of transportation advocates across North America. Some of the local advocacy wins I've been a part of while writing this book include fortifying a painted bike lane, getting safety measures installed to fix a deadly bus-only lane, and stopping a bus fare price increase. I also supported a regional funding measure for transit, got a local policy passed to create a permit process for community members who want to install benches at bus stops, pushed the members of Congress who represent my region to cosponsor transit operations funding legislation, put on about a dozen events as part of Bay Area Transit Month, and helped launch Southern California's inaugural Transit Week. I also led a project that got hundreds of political candidates on the record about transportation issues for 2024's primary and general elections. During that time, I also supported campaigns to keep Amtrak service in an East Bay community and to get a bus lane built in the South Bay. The reason I can do a lot is because everything I do, I do with others. There is a lot of transportation advocacy work to do, and when you team up with other people, you can get so much more done together than you could by yourself.

No one person can fight every transportation fight that we need to win. There are thousands of Main Streets in America, and I bet each one would be better with a protected bike lane and more bus service.[10] Every Main Street change involves its own campaign, and each campaign needs lots of people involved to win. With over ninety thousand local governmental jurisdictions in the United States, we need hundreds of thousands of transportation organizers focused on making our communities better.[11] Our movement needs you.

While this book is about encouraging you to take action, I promise I won't try to scare you into it. This book isn't about being miserable; it's about fixing the things that make us miserable. There is already an ocean of content dedicated to the problems humanity faces, which can fill people with anxiety. I won't try to motivate you by repeating the horrors covered in so many documentaries, newspapers, exposés, or Intergovernmental Panel on Climate Change reports. I won't delve into the time

I was hit by a car while biking as a teen, nor the vigils I have held with grieving neighbors who lost loved ones to traffic violence.

But if you do need some motivation to get started, you can search online for "traffic fatalities in my town." Or take a long walk; if you are currently able-bodied and child-free, bring a suitcase, folding shopping cart, or stroller with you to get a sense of how others may experience your streets. Or take the bus to run a series of time-sensitive errands. If you have a small child, go for a short bike ride with them. Take a long bike ride by yourself. Your lived experience will fire you up far more than any story or statistic will, and motivation is waiting for you just outside your front door. Every unpleasant car-dominated space you've been in, car crash you've heard about, or traffic jam you've been part of is a problem of the status quo. Every time you have written off a frustrating, scary, challenging, depressing, or enraging transportation-related moment of your life as "that's just the way things are" is a time you have tried to make peace with the failings of the status quo.

Instead of using fear or anger to tempt you to take action, I offer a special sort of hope. As Rebecca Solnit says in her book *Hope in the Dark*, "Hope is not a lottery ticket you can sit on the sofa and clutch, feeling lucky. It is an axe you break down doors with in an emergency. Hope should shove you out the door."[12] I believe that the hope-axe comes from two things: knowing that what you want is possible and knowing how to make it reality. This book is here to give you that hope, show you how to use it, and help you have an easier time waging your transportation-related campaigns for a better future.

Transportation Advocacy Is Constant and Everywhere

In transportation advocacy, the political battleground is everywhere at every moment and involves everyone. That big window of opportunity puts organizers in an astonishingly powerful position. For transportation advocates, when we pick a goal or a problem to fix, it can be really easy to find the people who care about it and connect with them when they care about it the most, which later chapters cover in detail.

For example, one night in 2023, I got dozens of people who were out clubbing to stop and sign a street safety petition. I did it by standing at a dangerous intersection between party spots and talking with people right after they were almost hit by car drivers. Before they started crossing the street, they were likely just thinking about the fun night ahead of them. But after that experience, they were very open to learning about how our city could make our streets safer. It helped that I wore a high-visibility construction vest and a friendly demeanor. After they were nearly hit and safely got to my side of the sidewalk, I would put a flyer near their hand and say something affirming and empowering like, "Oh jeez, that was scary. I'm glad you're okay. The city really needs to fix dangerous streets like this. Here's a petition about that; you just need to scan the QR code and bam, you've added your name and are ready to go clubbing. Great outfit by the way!" I recognized their immediate lived experience and gave them a near-frictionless way to take action to fix their problem.

As transportation advocates, we can connect most moments into the political point we want to make. For example, the conventional wisdom is that people are too busy to care about politics on a Friday night and that most people aren't that interested in street safety. But as transportation advocates, we can buck the conventional wisdom and have great success if we are strategic. Being audacious and friendly helps too.

Opportunities to shift our transportation politics are everywhere, and so are stories about how change is made. When people are shown advocacy in the news or in movies, they often only see hyper-visible actions like protests, sit-ins, petition deliveries, and street theater. Those are absolutely vital elements of success, and chapter 7 details how you can deploy them, but there is so much more that goes into making campaigns successful. This book will help strengthen your advocacy by explaining what goes into all of that behind-the-scenes work and how it connects to what goes on in public.

For example, in 2023, when a pro-transit coalition of diverse organizations got California Governor Gavin Newsom to reverse $2 billion in proposed transit funding cuts and provide over $1 billion in additional funding, it took pretty much every tool in the toolbox. Building power for that effort took lots of coalition building, education work, flyering, fundraising, lobbying, researching, strategizing, message crafting, and much more. At the same time, we put on disruptive and hyper-visible actions, which supercharged the campaign and put an international spotlight on the issue when it was most needed. One of those actions was a "transit funeral," where we carried mock coffins with huge cardboard trains in the streets of downtown Oakland, then on BART and into San Francisco. That action even got the British magazine *The Economist* to cheekily admit, "Sometimes, it turns out, protests work."[13]

Nearly everything you need to know in order to do the same for your community, city, or state is in this book. This book can help you win an amazing variety of changes and help you weather the defeats along the way. You might lose, but you won't fail: The only way to fail in organizing is by giving up. As long as you are learning from your experiences, growing, and continuing to fight, you are succeeding.

In fact, this book exists largely because of a fight I lost. A few years ago, I led a three-year quest to win a bus-only lane on the San Francisco–Oakland Bay Bridge and its three highway approaches. Our campaign came tantalizingly close to victory: We got a bill introduced and it passed the state senate. But a global pandemic and the promotion of two of our champion policymakers out of the legislature hobbled the effort, and eventually it was killed in a committee. While that defeat still chafes me, that campaign was one of the core initial organizing efforts that helped form Transbay Coalition, which has since been my organizing home in the region. Through that effort, I built relationships and learned lessons that have been central to all of my transit-related organizing since then.

No advocate who is doing bold things is undefeated. I won't sugarcoat it: You will lose sometimes. I won't lie to you and say, "Jump in, the water is fine." The water is not fine. I want you to jump in anyway.

What's Ahead

This book will help you be as successful as possible while minimizing unnecessary difficulty. You can read it cover to cover or skip around, reading the chapters in the order that sticks out to you. Either way, this book is here to be a resource for you.

This book is for beginners and mid-level activists who want to win transportation changes that make it easier to get around without a car. Veteran organizers who learned their craft from experience may also appreciate this book's attempt to make the often-chaotic world of activism more coherent. If I had this book when I was starting out, I would have jumped years ahead in my political change-making experience. I hope it saves you a lot of time, headaches, and heartaches. As the Bicycle Alliance of Minnesota's executive director Michael Wojcik says: "Better than learning from your mistakes is learning from other people's mistakes."[14]

This book guides you through embracing the fight, planning it out, and taking action. Each chapter ends with a handful of Action Points with exercises to help you apply the chapter's lessons. Chapter 1 answers our community's frequent questions about why we haven't made the transportation progress we see in other places around the world. It drills deeper into the ideas from this introduction to help readers get comfortable with embracing politics and see our reality more clearly. Chapter 1 details how wanting to cross the street safely is in fact a radical desire in America today, how being apolitical is not possible, and how to use that truth to better aim your energies.

The middle of the book will help you plan out your fight. Chapter 2 helps you turn your general dream into a specific campaign to make things better. Our hopes and advocacy also do not exist in a vacuum, so chapter 3 helps readers assess their unique situation and tailor their advocacy to it. It will also guide you through the fact that your transportation advocacy exists within a greater context of US politics, which often includes painful realities and historical traumas. The past is still very present and it impacts your advocacy, so chapter 3 will help you better navigate that.

The last and largest part of the book dives more specifically into the "how." It walks readers through how to build and deploy political power in different ways. A campaign can seem like a lot to jump into and take on alone, but you are not alone. Chapter 4 focuses on growing your allied forces of fellow transportation advocates and how to collaborate so you can win. Chapter 5 expands into building larger coalitions with all sorts of groups that are already working on these and related issues, including disability justice groups, immigrant rights groups, racial justice groups, unions, business associations, environmental groups, climate groups, civic associations, and other organizations. Chapter 6 explains how outside advocates and political insiders can work together to win their shared goals. Chapter 7 walks through which actions you can use as stepping stones to get to those goals and how to take those steps, such as petitioning, working with reporters, and creating electoral consequences for the decision-makers you seek to sway.

The book concludes with recommendations for handling what happens after a campaign, preparing for the next one, and shaping your advocacy to last a lifetime. While a particular transportation campaign may come to an end, transportation advocacy never does.

Jumping into the Unknown

It is possible to win a better world, but that takes work. The work is not always easy, fun, or glamorous, and it is rarely financially rewarding, but it is always important. I hope this book makes it easier for you to do whatever part of that work you set out to do. I hope you win. And for the times you do not win, I hope this book—along with the joy, community, and meaning that suffuse transportation organizing—helps you be brave and resilient enough to innovate and try again.

This book is me betting on you. I am counting on you too. Your community and our planet need you to win. No one has to be ready or perfect to get started, you just need to start. And guess what—you have already started. So, roll up your sleeves: Let's get political, let's fight, and let's win.

CHAPTER 1

Politics Isn't a Dirty Word

For advocacy, you don't need any degree. You don't need any papers. You don't need any of that. You get together with people who also share the same concerns as you and you figure out how to bring more people into this, and together you win the change you want.—Bakari Height, MARTA Army cofounder and former transportation planner[1]

You can do politics. Many people may be intimidated by politics or dislike it because they think that "politics" means Republicans versus Democrats or because our political situation today is a bit heated (to put it mildly). However, the struggle between political parties is just a subset of politics: partisan politics. Politics is so much bigger than that—it's the process of people shaping each other's lives, whether in workplaces, families, governments, or beyond. Our transportation system is part of this process. People create our transportation system, which in turn thoroughly affects everyone's lives, so transportation issues are inherently political.

Of course, transportation advocates sometimes have to deal with partisan politics. For example, in 2015, the Bicycle Coalition of Maine had to adapt its approach to work in a hyper-partisan environment. Maine's

Republican governor staunchly refused to pass any legislation introduced by Democrats, so the group focused its campaign on something that would appeal to a Republican lawmaker: a bill that emphasized the responsibilities and rights of bicyclists and pedestrians.[2] The coalition worked with a Republican lawmaker to introduce the bill, which the governor ended up signing into law.[3] They won by successfully navigating their political context rather than pretending their transportation goals were somehow separate from politics. Winning transportation change is a lot easier when transportation advocates recognize the political nature of their work, so this chapter focuses on laying that foundation.

Politics Is About People

People built our transportation system, and people are trying to either change it or keep things the way they are. Elected officials, government staffers, business owners, workers, community leaders—they are all people, just like you. Their transportation-related decisions affect the world around them, and we can influence those decisions.

Regular people make political transportation decisions all the time without realizing it. For example, when a person in a car-dependent place decides to go anywhere, they may not feel like they are making a transportation choice, and they may not be aware of how their choice affects others. From their perspective, they are not choosing to drive to a destination; they are just choosing to go there, and they may feel like a car is their only option.

In the United States, car dependency is currently the status quo. Conversely, in transit-friendly places like the Netherlands or South Korea, the status quo supports the development of more transit. That doesn't mean it's apolitical to expand transit in those areas; it means that the pro-transit side has so thoroughly won the political fight that abundant, high-quality transit is considered normal.

Advocates for better transit, biking, and street safety in the US often have to put in a lot of work because challenging the status quo is hard. It's easier to accept the systems you are operating within rather than push to change them. When people are used to something, they may not even realize that they can or should change it. For example, every single day on local news radio stations across the country, announcers talk about traffic. As part of those radio traffic updates, announcers often comment about highway backups due to car crashes. If you're listening to the report while you are driving, you just heard that a person in your area may have died a few moments ago while doing the same thing you are doing right now. You might even drive past the wreckage. That was a person's life. A life just as important as yours, and it could just as easily have been you. That is a hard reality to sit with. It is much easier to chalk that up to "that's how things are" and accept or ignore the costs of our car-centric status quo than it is to reject or work to change the status quo.

Every aspect of our transportation system is inherently political—even when it doesn't look like it's doing anything at all. Politics and how it shapes the world is often invisible. For example, you can't physically see the apparatus of political power that creates and maintains parking spots, nor can you see parking's full impacts on society. As Donald Shoup points out in *The High Cost of Free Parking*, building a parking spot costs tens of thousands of dollars. Shoup writes: "If drivers don't pay for parking, who does? Everyone does, even if they don't drive. Initially the developer pays for the required parking, but soon the tenants do, and then their customers, and so on, until the cost of parking has diffused everywhere in the economy."[4]

Additionally, parking spots have major environmental costs to society beyond their financial costs. If someone is unaware of parking's cost to society, they may incorrectly view parking as apolitical, rather than seeing how it is a product of human decisions and how it affects society. Cars and parking are so enmeshed in our current transportation system that efforts to shift things away from them usually involve a power struggle. In fact, attempts to change our transportation system are often viewed as radical.

Transportation Politics Is Radical

Being radical means wanting reality to change significantly. Safe streets, protected bike lane networks, and frequent transit are radical departures from our status quo. Cars are so dominant in the United States that 87 percent of daily trips take place in a private vehicle.[5] It is statistically weird for an adult in the US to leave their home and go to work without using a car. According to a 2021 Census report, "The Northeast had the highest share of workers who commuted by transit, at 14.3%, followed by the West (4.4%), the Midwest (3.0%), and the South (2.0%)."[6] A 2023 nationwide transportation study said that with 1.3 percent of all commute trips happening by bike, Oregon was the state with the highest share of bike commuting.[7] Given these percentages, "it's a powerful statement to ride your bike anywhere," said Kalli Krumpos of the Washington Area Bicyclist Association.[8] She told me that "it can be an act of resistance to be on your bike."[9] To want a lot more people to bike or ride transit is to want society to be radically different.

It can be difficult for transportation advocates to internalize this truth. We tend to want pretty straightforward and reasonable things, so it can be hard to see our desires as radical. But it does take radical change to make it so that you can be safe biking around town, or you can take a train wherever you want to go, or your kid can walk to school without the threat of traffic violence. You aren't wrong to want these things; it's society that's wrong. Because of our current transportation system, tens of thousands of our neighbors die violent deaths on our roads each year, millions of people aren't able to get where they need to go, and hundreds of millions of people around the globe suffer the ravages of climate change. We transportation advocates are right to want radical changes to our deadly and broken transportation system. Given that our reality is catastrophic, it's good to want to divert from it!

Our status quo is so out of sync with the needs of our planet and the people who live on it that, as Naomi Klein says in her book *This Changes Everything: Capitalism vs. the Climate*, "there are no non-radical options left."[10] When we recognize that the shifts we want are radical, we can better understand that we will need to build a lot more political power to win, and we can plan accordingly. As mentioned in the introduction, advocates cannot get hundreds of billions of dollars to fund transit by asking nicely. We can only win if we are clear-eyed about what we are up against and if we have the power to back up our demands. When you have a realistic understanding that change is political and politics is about power, you can seriously examine the power you have, the power you can build, and the power you will need in order to win what you want. The rest of this book will help teach you how to build and wield that sort of power. Before we get to that, we need to face another hard truth.

Process Is Political

In transportation, there is no escaping politics. If you were to examine transportation questions on some "objective" or "technical" merit, you would almost always reach the conclusion that cars are not the best answer. However, the decisions that shape our world are not objective. There is no politics-free way to make a decision that impacts people. Even a "purely technical" decision-making process about transportation issues is political because it affects people's lives and because people are the ones who make the process and decide what to prioritize within it.

What Is a Process?

In transportation, we often deal with processes to make and enact decisions. A process may be determined by some outside authority or be self-imposed by a community. For example, the process for getting a speed bump in your community might require filling out an official application with a certain number of residents' signatures and submitting it to some committee. External rules may have shaped that process—like a state law requiring towns to get community input before they change roads—but the specifics are likely designed by the town itself.

Many communities' processes can impede transportation changes such as sidewalk expansions, protected bike lane additions, or transit line extensions. For example, the process to convert an intersection into a pedestrian plaza in your town is likely not an easy one. While there are rarely simple, predefined processes for implementing the changes we want to see, there are often established processes for doing things we don't want, such as tearing down homes to widen freeways. Winning the changes we want as transportation advocates can involve reforming old processes or creating new ones. Win a plaza conversion once and now there is a process for doing it a second time. Reform the housing removal process and you can stop a highway expansion.

Process as a Political Tool

Process adds layers of abstraction to political decisions. It distances the decision-maker from their decisions, which can be helpful for a decision-maker who wants to hide their attempt to kill a popular proposal. For example, since 2001, transit advocates in Atlanta have advanced a light-rail and walking trail project called the Beltline, which loops the city to connect many neighborhoods.[11] The walking trail has already been built, but the proposed light-rail—which has been key to the project since its inception—is stalled. Atlanta Mayor Andre Dickens, who holds enormous sway over the Beltline light-rail's future, has been using process as a tool to stop the project while creating an illusion of impartiality.

For years, numerous studies have consistently affirmed the importance and technical feasibility of light-rail on the Beltline.[12] However, when asked in a 2024 interview about the project, Mayor Dickens brought up "the need" for another study before the light-rail can proceed.[13] He said, "We are still looking at how to make sure that we can fully vet this process. . . . Do we want it to be on rails, do we want it to be on rubber tires, do we want small pods, or do we want to leave this as a walking trail?"[14] Pushing for yet another study is a way to prevent the project from moving forward. Even more alarming, the mayor's statement introduces the prospect of building no transit at all. I don't know for sure why the mayor would do such a thing, but the people in affluent areas who have been lobbying against the light-rail seem to be happy with the mayor's actions. Considering that a light-rail line has always been central to the Atlanta Beltline project, the mayor would cause an uproar if he said outright that he wants to kill the project. Politicians who want to do something unpopular often use process to pretend the matter is out of their hands.

When politicians try to escape accountability by pointing to engineering or technical planning processes, it puts transportation professionals in an awkward position. Transportation professionals are supposed to be apolitical actors who carry out the will of elected officials and the community. But appearing to be apolitical does not eliminate biases; it just hides them. When I interviewed Josh, the urban planner behind the YouTube channel Radical Planning, he said, "It's kind of taboo to be a planner and admit that your own actions are political. . . . We can kind of exculpate ourselves from advancing that plan through the political realm."[15] However, he said, "planning is political at every stage."

Josh gave an example: "Sometimes [politicians] just give [government staffers] a list of organizations that they think should be key stakeholders: the groups that they are interested in, the ones they want you to make sure are moved to the front above the general public. That ends up giving particular groups an outsized voice in the process."[16]

Josh also shared an example of a county staffer who was asked to make a survey about widening a road in a scenic corridor. The county politicians were very clear that they wanted to widen the road regardless of public opinion, "so the planner made a survey where every answer would be positive," Josh said. "The questions were things like, 'Which do you like more?' And it wouldn't be a choice between widening a road and not widening a road, it would be something like widening the road to four lanes or four lanes and a median."[17]

When the decision-making process blocks out options from even being considered, as was the case with the survey Josh mentioned, it channels the conversation in a certain direction. This can be used to justify almost anything, like bulldozing homes to build a freeway. On the other hand, we can make processes that justify bulldozing freeways to build homes. Process is a tool, like a screwdriver or a knife. It isn't inherently good or bad, but it is political.

To readers who are professionals in the transportation space and are nervous about being "political" or "an activist," you are already political. You are already actively shaping the world to be a certain way, so you are already an activist, and you have power you can wield. Josh says, "You can, as the planner, also highlight what you think is important. If you knew anecdotally that an intersection was dangerous and you have the data to show that, then there isn't anything wrong with just adding that data point to a report on the area even if no one else asked you to."[18] You can find more detail on strategies transportation professionals and advocates can use to move things in the direction they want in chapter 6.

Fear, Anger, and Getting Political

Transportation issues are some of the most visible ways that governments touch our lives. However, it can be hard for the average person to stay up to date and engaged in these decision-making processes. When someone thinks that an important decision about their life is being made without them, they may get upset, especially if they think that decision will hurt them. Transportation changes can feel like they are being done *to* a community rather than *for* or *with* a community. Clear communication and community engagement can preempt a lot of these concerns, but you will always be able to find people who object to change.

Eric Rogers of the Kansas City group BikeWalkKC says, "For the people who are scared of change, that fear is often a barrier to their thinking about how they could benefit directly or indirectly from that change."[19] That fear comes from somewhere. Some people may lose their job if a change to their transportation situation makes them late to work one more time. Some people physically cannot stand to wait for a bus, and some people drive to avoid harassment on the street or on transit. Often people in these situations do not have the means or the time to consider trying something different. Whether or not they would benefit from a change, their situation is so precarious that they are not interested in rolling the dice to see if the change you want could help them. Chapter 3 covers understanding and navigating your community's context in more depth so you can better connect with people even if they have hesitations.

At the same time, transportation advocates need to understand that our vocal opposition often argues in bad faith. Opponents to your campaign can form up because they fear change, and they may stoke fears (valid or not) to stop you. For example, the "No on San Francisco's Proposition K" campaign tried to stop the conversion of a beachfront highway into a park. The No on K campaign was so enraged at the idea of a little-used road being turned into a new park, they held an aggressive protest at a playground where the Yes on K campaign was planning a public Q&A session for families. Due to this intimidation, the Yes on K campaign had to cancel their event, stating: "Prop K opponents showed up with a bullhorn and were harassing attendees. This isn't something we want to put families through. Stay tuned for a future events [sic] to learn more about Prop K."[20]

Unfortunately, this is not an isolated incident. People defending the car-centric status quo sometimes use aggressive tactics to try to

Figure 1.1. "No on Prop K" supporters protesting at a playground where the "Yes on Prop K" campaign was planning to host a family-friendly educational event. *Credit:* Yes on Prop K campaign

intimidate community members. Often, this kind of opposition cannot be appeased, but we can build power, organize, and win anyway. In the "Prop K" example, the people promoting the park won, the bullies lost, and the highway is now a car-free place for all to enjoy. You may encounter opposition, but you can win in spite of it.

The Journey from Where You Are to Where You Need to Be

When we accept that transportation-related desires are political and often radical, we can view our desires as what they are: political struggles. That understanding makes it easier to translate our dreams into the plans and actions needed to win. The next chapter covers the different pathways you can take in order to bring your desired change into reality.

Action Points

1) Check your local news for a story about a proposed transportation change in your area. See if you can find out:
   a) Who are some of the people supporting the change?
   b) Who actively opposes it or doesn't like it?
   c) Which of those people do you think has more political power and why?
2) For that proposed transportation change in your area, look around to see what stage of the decision-making process it is in. That information may be in the article or in other news about the proposal, or you may need to check if the responsible governing agency has that information online. **Bonus** What is the next step if the proposal makes it through this step?
3) Think of a transportation change you want. Who would benefit from it? Who might see themselves as "losing" if it happened?

CHAPTER 2

Picking Your Battles and Outlining Your Campaign

This [new city policy] was the only way to slowly start to build out a connected sidewalk network, which is not enough, but it was a start. And now we are at risk of losing that, so we're gearing up for a fight [to defend it].—Ines Sigel, LINK Houston[1]

One good thing about the American transportation system is that there are a lot of ways to make it better. Like much of America, Houston, Texas, is a place where it's hard to get around without a car. Local transportation activists, including the group LINK Houston, have been waging a number of campaigns to fix that. In 2024, LINK Houston successfully defended a city policy that required developers to either build sidewalks as part of their projects or pay into a citywide sidewalk construction fund. The group, whose mission is to advance "a robust and equitable transportation network so that all people can reach opportunity," chose to mount a campaign to protect sidewalks from the new city administration's attacks because, as deputy executive director Ines Sigel said, "sidewalks are part of a well-connected public transit system.[2]

Like LINK Houston, you may have a wide set of values you bring to your transportation advocacy. You need to translate them into concrete campaigns in order to win specific changes. This chapter will help you convert your values into actionable campaigns with different pathways to your destination. As explained in the introduction, this book won't tell you which dreams to dream—that's up to you. Whatever your dream is, this chapter will help you translate it into a clear objective you can build a campaign around. This chapter will illustrate the steps between envisioning something, figuring out who can officially make it happen, and then getting it implemented in the real world.

Articulating What You Want

Whether you are a first-time advocate, a veteran transportation activist, an elected official, or a government agency staffer, translating your transportation dream into a winnable campaign requires getting specific about what you want. Since there are so many transportation changes to want, table 2.1 presents a few questions you can ask yourself to focus your attention.

When you have a clearer understanding of what you want, it's easier to think about which transportation campaigns would be needed to make that happen. You may find that you want some epic shifts to our transportation system as well as tiny changes that would make your life a bit more convenient. Although the fundamentals of effective campaigns are similar regardless of scale, there are some key differences between big and small fights.

Picking a Big Fight

It's not inherently harder to win a bigger demand than a smaller demand. In fact, one of the best ways to win something is to demand a lot and then settle for as much as you can get. If you ask for something and are met with indifference, it can be tempting to shrink your demands in response. Don't. In politics, you almost always get less than what you

Table 2.1. Generating Rough Ideas for Transportation Campaigns

Clarifying question	*Example*
What's a pain point you want to solve?	"It's frustrating having to use a car to get to the park; I want to be able to get to the park without a car."
If you could have one transportation wish magically granted, what would it be?	"I wish I never had to check when the next bus was coming because they were running so frequently."
What is something that is under attack that you care about?	"They want to get rid of my bus line and I want to keep it."
What's something that feels like it should be a commonsense, easy change to enact?	"I can't believe there isn't bike parking at my local grocery store; that should be easy to make happen, right?"
What's a small change that would make you really happy?	"I would love it if my street became a cul-de-sac with cut-throughs so cars couldn't get through it but people could."

ask for, so if you ask for less, you will get a lot less. Instead, be bold and campaign for more.

When you demand more, you shift the "Overton window," which is the range of what the mainstream community considers politically reasonable. When politicians consider which laws to introduce, they tend to think about what their allies and the general public would support. If a politician thinks they could get your idea passed into law, then they will be more open to it. As transportation activists, our campaigns can shift what people consider reasonable. When we shift the Overton window by demanding a lot of change and fighting for it, we move things in our direction. The new "reasonable compromise" position is one where we end up with more than where we first started.

For example, asking for a bench at your bus stop is within the current Overton window: Bus stops generally have benches, so it's reasonable to ask for one. Yet many bus stops still don't have benches even after advocates request them. When your request for a bench is turned down, you could shrink back and try to win something smaller, or you could get bolder and campaign for a bench at *every* bus stop. Your new demand—and the campaign to back it up—changes what would be considered a reasonable compromise. The people in charge could respond by increasing the city's budget for installing benches at bus stops or committing to put benches at the most-used bus stops within a certain number of years. If you push for a big goal, you likely won't win it outright, but you can put yourself in a position to "settle" for winning something that moves you toward your new goal, and maybe you'll even win the smaller thing you wanted in the first place. Take the win, make sure it gets implemented, celebrate it when it does, and then campaign for more.

You can shift the Overton window in a variety of ways, such as by demanding a faster rate of change or shifting what you demand. However, keep your demands within the realm of reality by considering what your potential allies might think of as the far end of reasonable. Having massage chairs at every bus stop is technically possible, but it would likely be considered unreasonable by even your staunchest allies.

A benefit of campaigning to shift the Overton window is that even if you technically lose, you can still come out ahead. Even if you don't win anything yet from the relevant decision-maker, you may have successfully injected the concept into the collective conversation, built a base of supporters, and created new relationships with decision-makers that make the next fight easier. The progress we make opens up larger possibilities, which is vital considering the long timelines transportation activists often operate in. Michael Wojcik, executive director of the Bicycle Alliance of Minnesota and a former city councilmember, puts it succinctly: "Sometimes you introduce a bill to get it passed. Sometimes you introduce a bill to get it passed in ten years."[3] The next time around, you might have better luck since you will have gotten people more used to the idea and built more organizational power compared to your first campaign. Picking big fights to shift the Overton window is an excellent way to chip away at the status quo and steadily build the world we want.

Picking a Small Fight

Of course, not every fight you pick has to be epic. Smaller fights can tee up larger wins and, collectively, they can achieve big things. While this book focuses on pushing governmental decision-makers, many small transportation wins can be scored outside of government. For example, you could campaign to get your local festival to set up a bike valet. You may choose to target an array of other entities like community members, businesses, and organizations to get them to be more supportive of transit, biking, and walking. In this book, the implied decision-maker is a government official, but the lessons generally translate to these non-governmental actors as well.

In the world of government, you can shrink the size of your fight by campaigning for policies that are recommendations rather than mandates, or pilot projects rather than full installs. Abbey Seitz, the director of transportation equity for Hawaiʻi Appleseed Center for Law and Economic Justice, explains, "Quick-build projects, even if they're on a smaller scale, can make a huge difference in helping open people's minds." Even people who oppose projects at first might change their minds once they can actually witness the results from a pilot project or a quick build that uses materials like plastic rather than concrete. "Just to see it, even on a small scale, is really impactful," she says.[4]

Small wins are also good in their own right. For example, in 2013, I won new bike parking racks installed in the fare-gated area of my local train station by politely pestering the transit director on social media. It was a small victory and one that didn't take a lot of pushing, since the target decision-maker was a bike fan herself. Now there is a bike rack in an area where there wasn't one before—one less problem in the world.

Small victories can also collectively achieve big things. In 2020, Safe Routes to School advocate Megan Ramey started small with, as she describes it, a "little bike train that could" in Hood River, Oregon.[5] The bike parade she organized with the local elementary school principal was a small victory that helped "break the vicious chicken-egg cycle with no children walking or biking, leading to no political support for safe routes to school." After the bike train, Ramey says, they "invested in one-on-one relationships with the students, taught them how to bike, and took group rides and walks in the street."[6] These steps are victories in their own right, and they built local support for installing demonstration projects—jump-starting a virtuous cycle of getting more kids biking, garnering more political support, and winning more safety improvements.

Over the next two years, the Safe Routes to School coalition's small victories added up, helping them win twenty-one grants totaling $10 million for bike education programs and infrastructure in the community, and getting over one thousand kids across five elementary schools and two middle schools walking and biking to school in Hood River County. What started with a little bike train ended up reshaping transportation for a generation of children in the county—and the advocates are still going strong.

Winning Change Takes Progress on Multiple Fronts

What you want as a transportation advocate will require progress on different pathways. For the purpose of clarity, this chapter categorizes these paths into three types of campaigns: culture, policy, and budget. These types of campaigns can fuse into each other, particularly when it comes to winning infrastructure or transit service changes. For example, if you want a car-free plaza in your town, you will need to win a *culture* shift so the community supports and protects it from backlash, the *policy* that approves it, and the *budget* to fund and maintain it. The next section walks through the distinct abilities and limitations of these campaign types so that you can better evaluate how to use them to make your vision a reality.

Culture Fights

Similar to the Overton window, culture is what's considered normal and expected in a community. It is colloquially described as "what we do around here." When you win a culture fight, you win the battle of hearts and minds, reshaping the emotional landscape around your issue, which makes it easier to win more tangible changes later on. Like Megan Ramey's success in Hood River to shift the culture by getting kids on bikes, a culture-shifting effort can focus on a community. It can also focus on an individual. For example, if you get a government official to participate in Week Without Driving—the nationwide event organized each fall by America Walks and Disability Rights Washington—it will help open that official's eyes, and hopefully their heart, to the experience of nondrivers. This may make an official more likely to work with you on your priorities.

Our transportation system shapes and is shaped by our culture. When governments build freeways and sprawling suburbs, they foster a car-centric transportation culture. When we elevate the visibility of transit riders, pedestrians, and people on bikes, we build cultural power and can have an easier time winning changes to our transportation system.

A bike train or "bike bus" is a powerful tool for culture fights and is worth examining further. A bike bus or train is essentially a bike parade to school. An adult on a bike acts as the ride leader, going along a predefined route so kids and their grown-ups can join on their own bikes when the group rolls by. In putting together a bike bus, organizers explicitly change "what we do around here," because now kids biking to school is part of "what we do around here." This phenomenon is written about extensively in the world of political organizing theory, and it is referred to as "prefigurative politics." Changing the culture is important on its own, and it opens the door to all sorts of other things, such as communal demand for protected bike lanes to help keep kids safe. In the "Barcelona Declaration," bike bus organizers and participants at the 2023 Bike Bus Summit in Barcelona, Spain, wrote: "#BikeBus is joy and freedom. Community bike rides to school make kids happier, more awake and ready to learn. Our community becomes more connected and resilient. We demonstrate that our streets can be for children too. As a #BikeBus community, we demand that our political leaders prioritize urban space and resources for child friendly, healthy, and safer streets."[7]

A great part about being a transportation advocate is that you have a lot of tools to creatively wage culture fights. You can do it through hosting parties like group ride-alongs on transit, block parties where you close the street, or events explicitly themed around transportation—like Park(ing) Day, when folks convert parking spots to parklets. When we show that there are other ways to get around or to use space typically devoted to cars, we shift transportation culture. Getting an event venue to include a "how to get here by transit" section on their website is a win. Getting your friends to consider going out to a place that's walkable rather than requiring a drive can be a win too.

Culture fights can focus on getting people to adopt new habits, like riding the bus more often, as well as stopping certain behaviors. As transportation advocates, we can pick "negative" culture fights to try to stigmatize behaviors that are currently considered acceptable, such as the effort to stigmatize drunk driving, which helped reduce drunk driving deaths per capita by 55 percent since 1982.[8]

Negative culture fights mainly involve leveraging moral authority to set a standard of behavior and using shame to get others to follow suit. If the people saying "we don't do that around here" aren't respected people within your culture, they'll be ignored. A big part of why Mothers

Against Drunk Driving was so successful in passing anti–drunk driving laws stems from the fact that they leveraged the cultural legitimacy of mothers and parents who lost loved ones to drunk driving to make the dangerous behavior taboo.

Positive culture fights are a bit easier (and more fun) since your actions say, "Here's what people do around here, and we are doing it." Kalli Krumpos of the Washington Area Bicyclist Association (WABA) explains how her group started a positive cultural push in response to local businesses' opposition to a bike lane proposal through its "I bike, I buy" campaign. WABA encouraged people to mention to staff at stores and restaurants that they arrived by bike. The group also gave bikers "I bike, I buy stuff" business cards with more information to leave at the places they shop.[9] Krumpos explained that the campaign "educates those businesses about the fact that many of their customers are not coming to them by car." So far, she says, "it's helped build business support for bike infrastructure, but it's a slow shift."[10]

In the world of transportation, shifting culture can make a huge difference to build support and soften opposition. However, culture campaigns can be kneecapped by bad policies and infrastructure. Bad transportation behavior often happens because infrastructure enables it. People still drive through red lights. Speeding drivers still kill people in neighborhoods with "drive like your kids live here" signs, and drivers still wrongly use bus-only lanes when the lanes lack separators. We can win a culture that disapproves of dangerous driving, but we need to use our additional tools to induce larger behavioral change.

While culture isn't everything, campaigns that help shift culture can serve as foundations for larger victories. They can unlock virtuous cycles to get more people to join in on a behavior, normalizing and building political support for change. We can build the culture we want first and then leverage it to change our transportation system. That makes it easier to show policymakers that their constituents want the world to be a certain way, and they will in turn be more receptive to policies that affirm that culture.

Policy Fights

If culture is the general sense of "what we do around here," policies are the explicit rules. For example, it is generally culturally acceptable for a musician to play at a train station. Whether or not that is against the rules is a separate matter. A policy may dictate that all performers at a station must get prior approval from the transit agency.

Policy is an umbrella term, which can cover governmental laws that are enforced by the legal system, or rules made and upheld by other entities. For example, there may be a policy against street performers playing at your local transit station. That policy could be a rule from the transit agency that they only enforce when a station agent tells a street performer to leave if they behave obnoxiously. If the policy is a law from the city, it may be enforced with steep fines or even police. In either case, people made the policy, and people choose to uphold it. Advocates can change policies through policy fights. Whether it is a law or a rule, a campaign could aim to repeal it, reform it, or reduce the enforcement of it.

As a member of the general public, when you want to get a policy enacted, you may find that most policymaking spaces will not allow you to bring a proposal to a vote on your own. If you want to get a law enacted, you need a lawmaker to introduce it into the legislative process. If it is a rule for a transit agency, transportation department, or other entity, you need one of their internal rule-makers—like a board member or a key staffer—to introduce it.

Because there are so many types of policies and policymakers in the transportation space, this book tends to use the generic terms of "decision-maker" and "policymaker." This book also uses the words "politicians" and "lawmakers" to refer to decision-makers who have to run for office in an electoral process, but there are many decision-makers who are unelected. Later, this chapter will provide more details on which decision-makers have the power to do what. The more you strengthen relationships with policymakers, the more receptive they will be to introducing your proposed policy, or at least voting for it if one of their colleagues introduces it.

Getting Policymakers on Your Side

There are more than half a million elected officials in office across the United States, and most of them do not yet prioritize non-car transportation. There are generally two ways for transportation activists to get policymakers on our side. One is by putting transportation champions into public office. Similarly, having the ability to remove our opponents from office goes a long way in getting politicians on our side. As a movement, this is a weak spot for us. Anecdotally, I do not know of a politician in the US whose opposition to transit or street safety cost them an election.

Fortunately, we are seeing more candidates prioritize our issues enough to campaign on them when running for office, but only some of those candidates have won. Examples of a few wins from prior to 2025 include former Bay Area Rapid Transit (BART) board director Lateefah Simon, who won a seat in the US Congress; former BART board director Rebecca Saltzman, who won a seat on the El Cerrito City Council; and Jesse Brown, who won a seat on the Indianapolis City Council by centering transit in his campaign. While Simon and Saltzman were able to campaign on their past successes improving the transit agency, Brown ran on the promise of improving bus service if elected for the first time. Brown, a publicly avowed socialist, said, "When I ran for office, the first issue that I really approached my neighbors with was that our bus system needs to be better. . . . While I ran on many other issues, I introduced myself first and foremost as a bus rider."[11] Pro-transportation candidates can win if we help them, and the power we build in our transportation campaigns can also be used to support their electoral campaigns.

However, until we build the power needed to be able to change who is in office, we must rely on the second way to get policymakers on our side: building good relationships with them. Chapter 6 covers working with policymakers in more detail, and chapter 7 addresses how to get their attention in other ways.

To win a policy fight, it helps to have a policymaker on your side. It also helps to have a clearer understanding of the institutions involved in making policies and what goes into the policymaking process.

The Innards of Policy Fights

Policies don't just happen. Even laws to ban drunk driving or to require seat belts had to be fought for. Safety regulations—like the one that requires school bus drivers to stop at railroad crossings and confirm that the bus doors can open—are often said to be "written in blood" because they were passed in response to a fatal incident. Even these laws don't just happen; they have to be fought for, or else lawmakers will just send thoughts and prayers.

One important thing to keep in mind about persuading politicians: They care about what their constituents think, because their constituents voted them in and can vote them out. Getting multiple lawmakers to support your proposed policy requires building support for your proposal in different districts. If your representative introduces a bill and brings it to a vote, it will fail unless lawmakers from other districts vote for it. It's not enough to get just one lawmaker—like a city councilmember or state senator—to introduce your policy idea; you also need to get the majority of lawmakers on your side in order to pass a law. In our interview, Beth Osborne of the transportation and land use advocacy organization Smart Growth America noted that making a vote easy for an elected official "means having *their* constituents speak out to them about supporting the project."[12] We'll explore ways to build allies in other districts in the next few chapters.

When dealing with legislative bodies, it often matters which lawmaker is the author or sponsor of a bill. Even in legislative bodies that are nonpartisan, like many city councils or county boards of supervisors, there tends to be a political faction or alliance that sets the agenda.

In state or federal legislatures, political parties play a big role. Some policies will never get passed if they are introduced by someone in the party or faction that's not in control. As exemplified by the story of Maine's hyper-partisan governor in the previous chapter, one solution is to get a member of the controlling faction to introduce your idea. Another option is to build enough political strength to alter that balance of power. When all else fails, change the policy you are trying to pass, or try to get a different decision-maker to pass something similar that is within their power. If you can't win at your state legislature, try your city council—and vice versa.

In addition to legislatures, government agencies also set policies, but their inner workings can be a little more opaque. A main difference between agencies and legislatures is that agencies are more insulated from public opinion, which can make it harder for advocates to get heard. That partly stems from the fact that agencies—like Departments of Transportation or Public Works—are administrative bodies, where decision-makers are appointed rather than elected. Sometimes there is an official process for agencies to receive public input, like a hearing or public survey. You can apply pressure at those venues, for example by bringing supporters to the hearing to give public comment. Even if there is not an official public comment process, you can still pressure agencies in a variety of ways, which chapter 6 covers in more detail. One of the most important reasons to engage with agencies is that they often implement transportation policy and have a lot of decision-making power over how to do so. Later on, this chapter will detail the transportation-related powers of the different branches of government.

Policies About Policy

There are so many policies that there are even policies about how policies are made or how budgets are set. As mentioned in chapter 1, policies can be set by processes—and in those instances, changing the processes will produce different policies. When you change the policymaking process, you can usher in a shocking amount of change.

For example, traffic studies inform how traffic policies are made, and "a poorly designed traffic study can lead to no action or changes that increase speeding," says Ride Illinois's David Simmons. If we change policies so that traffic studies put a higher value on saving lives, then we will get traffic studies that recommend more effective life-saving interventions, and in turn change policies around traffic itself. Simmons explains, "If we change the way [engineers] come up with answers, we'll get better answers."[13] While processes may seem dry, they are all battlefields.

A particularly esoteric type of process is the "regulatory process," which is how government agencies make policies. In essence, when elected officials pass laws, those laws leave a lot to interpretation, so agencies then make rules that—in theory—clarify the law and follow the spirit of it. Even in this seemingly mundane bureaucratic process, transportation advocates can win or lose big.

For example, Ride Illinois and its coalition partners masterfully engaged in a regulatory process to improve road safety around 2005. At the time, when the state paved road shoulders, there was no standard practice for where to put "rumble strips," a road design feature that alerts drivers when they drift out of their lane. Creating a rumble strip standardization process may seem boring and relatively apolitical, but even innocuous-seeming bureaucratic processes can potentially be sites of major political victories for transportation advocates. Seizing the opportunity to weigh in on this decision-making process, Ride Illinois and allies worked with the Illinois Department of Transportation (IDOT) to enact a new standard of rumble strips to the left of the shoulder. As Ride Illinois's executive director David Simmons put it, that change made it so "you have a de facto bike lane, and the standard trickles down to municipal standards too, so it'll slowly go out everywhere."[14] Though a rumble strip–protected bike lane is a far cry from the gold standard of protected bike lanes that are comfortable for riders of all ages and abilities, it provides more protection than a painted line.

IDOT didn't intend to create a process that would end up making hundreds of miles of semi-protected bike lanes; the department just wanted to standardize rumble strip installation practices. But Ride Illinois saw the opportunity for what it was, handled it deftly, and paved the way for a significant expansion of bike-friendlier infrastructure in the state.

Additionally, you can fight to change processes so they have fewer hurdles, which makes it easier for you to win what you want. For example, the advocacy group Californians for Electric Rail worked with Assemblymember Alex Lee in 2024 to pass a bill that would exempt rail electrification projects from certain regulations in order to speed up future projects. They did this in response to the wealthy enclave of Atherton abusing the project development process to delay the electrification of the California regional rail between San José and San Francisco. The delay lasted three years and caused the project cost to grow by roughly 25 percent.[15] This did serious damage, so rail advocates changed the process to prevent future abuses.

You can campaign to remove hurdles for the things you like, or you can add hurdles to slow down the things you don't want. In response to "a council president who was against bike lanes and introduced an ordinance so that whenever bike lanes went in there had to be a community meeting ahead of time to let people know," Detroit Greenways

Coalition's Todd Scott explains how their group got the city to enact a similar policy to slow down the city's bike lane removal process.[16] Now when the City of Detroit tries to remove a bike lane, they also have to hold a community meeting about it. The group couldn't stop the anti–bike lane policy, but at least they could slow down the bike lane removal process.

It Takes More Than Just Passing a Policy

When you plan out your campaign, keep in mind that transportation activists need to be vigilant to guide their wins through the implementation phase or else things may fall apart. Pittsburghers for Public Transit's Laura Chu Wiens gives an example from early on in the pandemic, when the group organized and won federal relief money for its transit agency. They weren't explicit about what the money should be used for, and "the transit agency banked that money, claiming to be 'fiscally responsible' while cutting desperately needed service and leaving people stranded," she said. "We felt deeply betrayed when they got about $400 million and they cut service and didn't provide fare relief." The transit agency effectively robbed the activists of the end result they were fighting for. Now, says Chu Wiens, "we do not advocate for anything for the transit agencies without tying it to specific solutions first."[17]

At the end of the day, your policy win is just ink on paper: It's the implementation that matters. If the people responsible for implementing the policy don't do it, you are in trouble. For example, even after the official commissioners approved the congestion charge for Manhattan south of 60th Street in 2024, New York Governor Kathy Hochul subverted the process, stepped in, and paused it for months on end. After significant pushback, she relented and became a champion of the policy. One of the best ways to make sure your policy gets implemented is by building a lot of support for it. Chapters 4 through 7 explain in more detail about how to build that support.

Implementation is especially vital when it comes to winning new infrastructure like a bus route, bike lane, or high-speed rail line. Infrastructure is the physical stuff of a community, like its roads and buildings, and it can be the systems a community depends on, like transit service. Winning new infrastructure takes the budget to pay for it, the policies that enable it, and the culture to demand it. Even then, you need to make sure it actually gets implemented, because your opposition may outright stop the project or delay it so much that the project dies a slow death. That often means that after you win your demand, there may be follow-up fights you also need to win. For example, if you want expanded bus service, you can get your transit agency to say they will run it, but if the transit agency can't hire enough bus operators to run the service, you still won't have the service you wanted.

One way to ensure policies get implemented is by attaching financial carrots or sticks to them. Offering financial rewards for going along with the policy, or withholding funds from entities who try to buck the policy, can go a long way when it comes to compliance. In order to win the funds you need, usually you have to win a distinct type of campaign: the budget fight.

Budget Fights

There is a cost to most of the transportation changes that you want. Even lowering the speed limit on a road involves paying for new signs and the labor costs for sign installation. Fortunately, governments have more than enough money to pay for everything you might want. For example, the federal government's budget is trillions of dollars. It regularly borrows trillions more, and debt isn't that big of a deal for the federal government as it has carried debt for nearly two centuries.[18] The price tag for any transportation project you could want is a drop in the bucket for the federal government.

State and local governments are more constrained, but they still have eye-popping budgets. In 2021, state governments collected $2.7 trillion in general revenues, and local governments collected $2 trillion.[19] Even a small local government has enough money to run frequent transit service and build quality people-centric transportation infrastructure. The United States is a fabulously wealthy country, and our federal, state, and local governments can pay for pretty much any transportation change they want. The issue is that they don't want to. That's why we need more transportation activists!

A pivotal fact about the government's money is that it isn't just sitting around waiting for you to ask for it. Governments have already decided what to spend their money on via their budgets. When elected officials say, "We don't have the budget," they are really saying, "We've already allocated the budget, and I don't care enough about your thing to remove funds from something else to give to you." The best time to get funding allocated to the transportation change you want is when the budget is being made, which generally happens every year or two. The administrative staffers at a governing body—like a city clerk—can help you get information about its budget process.

It's always helpful to identify where the money should come from, and fortunately, as transportation advocates, we have two gigantic piñatas of potential funding we can campaign to get money from: public safety and transportation. Governments spend the majority of their money on those exact issues, and while the changes we push for would improve our communities' public safety and transportation systems, we don't usually see that money.

To fix that discrepancy locally, when my city was redoing its budget in 2023, I led a campaign to shift a sliver of its police budget to the street safety budget. The proposal was well received, and over a thousand people signed on to the demand along with businesses, unions, justice organizations, disability justice groups, and houses of worship. Some people supported it because they wanted community-based safety solutions beyond policing, and some people supported it because traffic-calming infrastructure like speed bumps can free up police to do other things.[20] In the end, we won a slight increase in our city's street safety budget. Unfortunately, the police budget still got tens of millions of dollars added to it and other departments' budgets were cut. When we ask for more funding, we are inherently asking for something else to get less. Given that roughly twice as many people in the US are killed by traffic violence than are murdered each year, it is reasonable to ask our governments to shift some of their public safety budgets from policing to street safety infrastructure.[21] For context, one of the largest influxes of federal funds for street safety was $1 billion per year for five years; meanwhile, the United States spends nearly $300 billion per year on policing and incarceration.[22] Our country spends more than enough money to try and make our communities safer—by adjusting how we spend it, even a tiny bit, we could save tens of thousands of lives each year.

Even funds that are allocated for transportation-specific purposes could be better spent. For example, the state government of Texas already spends $32 billion each year on just one transportation technology: state highways.[23] That is more than enough money to build subways, rapid bus service, protected bike lanes, and a significant portion of a Texas high-speed rail network. For one-third of the cost of widening Interstate 35, the Austin metro area could complete the last 800 miles of a 1,200-mile bike network, points out Kelsey Huse, one of the founding board members of the Rethink35 campaign in Texas.[24] Similar to the question of public safety, the issue is not that Texas isn't spending enough money on transportation—it's that the government is spending its money on *automobile* transportation.

If you can't get enough money for what you want from the existing budget, you could campaign to bring in new money to help cover the costs. Transportation projects are often funded by a mix of local, county, state, and federal sources, so if your jurisdiction doesn't have the money to cover the full project cost, ask for funding help from a higher jurisdiction. Another way to help your community afford the transportation change you are fighting for is by campaigning for a new tax or bond to fund what you want.

Picking Your Budget Fight, Picking Your Opponents

Because winning funding may come at the expense of something else, budget fights are more likely to incite opposition, so pick your fight wisely. Pick a source of funds that will win you powerful allies, or only provoke opponents you are okay with provoking.

The worst fight to pick is cannibalizing the meager budget for people-centered transportation. Governments spend only crumbs on transit, active transportation, and street safety. Don't fight your fellow transportation advocates over scraps. At best, you'll win a slightly larger scrap and destroy relationships with your closest potential allies. Instead, band together to fight for a bigger collective piece of the pie.

You can also pick a negative budget fight to get someone to stop spending money on something you don't want. If you want to stop freeway expansion, you can campaign to eliminate the freeway expansion budget. A fun part about negative budget fights is you can also use them to tempt powerful allies to join your cause. In the freeway example, it might be ideal to shift freeway funds to transit, but that takes a huge amount of political power, because it is both anti-freeway and pro-transit. One way to stop a freeway expansion is by getting the government to spend the freeway funds on something else. For example, if you campaign to get funds shifted from being wasted on freeways to being invested in the public school system, you may attract some powerful allies.

When it comes to winning funding for transit agencies, infrastructure projects, or local Public Works Departments, you may want to fight for consistent funding sources or multiyear budgets so your funding doesn't run out. It's also better for your advocacy so you don't have to come back next year to fight for the funds again!

Budgets are just one of the powers legislators have over our transportation system. Different institutions have authority over different aspects of our transportation system; you may need to win across these arenas. A key step to planning out your campaign is to find out who actually has the power to give you what you want.

Who You Are Demanding Change From

A natural advantage we have as transportation advocates is that implementing transportation solutions is a relatively structured process. In the case of rail transit, says Irene Fernando, a county commissioner of Minnesota's Hennepin County, "There are only so many ways you get publicly funded and publicly governed rail."[25] There are also only so many decision-makers who can make it happen. A quick transportation civics lesson will help highlight who can do what in the different branches of the government, as well as government departments and agencies.

The US Constitution established the legal framework that separated out three branches of government and their powers. The legislative branch makes laws and sets budgets, the executive branch implements the laws, and the judiciary branch settles disputes about the law. This happens at the federal, state, and local levels. For example, the legislative branch at the federal level is the House of Representatives and the Senate, while at the state level it is state legislatures, and at the local level it is town or city councils.

Transportation advocates also regularly deal with government agencies like Departments of Transportation, which make all sorts of regulations within their jurisdictions. The agencies are typically established, empowered, and funded by the legislative branch but overseen by the executive branch. The executive branch—mayors, governors, or the president—appoints agency heads. Sometimes the legislative branch has to approve executive branch appointments. States, territories, counties, cities, and towns have their own constitutions or charters, as well as their own lawmakers and government agencies. In the areas within a county that are not part of a town—the "unincorporated" areas—the county government is the legislative body.

Transportation advocates also deal with two special types of governing bodies. One type is Metropolitan Planning Organizations (MPOs), which are federally mandated regional transportation planning agencies made up of local officials. MPOs decide where to direct the federal funds they receive, help coordinate between governments in the region, and make plans focused on meeting the region's future transportation needs.

The second type of special governing body you might deal with is a transit agency, which runs transit service in a given area. This is distinct from a Department of Transportation, which is responsible for the roads, highways, and other transportation routes in an area. Transit agencies can be independent agencies that are wholly separated from a city or state government. For example, the Utah Transit Authority, which runs transit service in Salt Lake City, Provo, and Ogden, is separate from Utah's Department of Transportation and Salt Lake City's Transportation Division. Like many transit agencies, the Utah Transit Authority has its own board of trustees and staff, who do not necessarily directly report to any elected official—though they may have been appointed by one. However, sometimes a transit agency is a sub-agency of a city or state's Department of Transportation, like the Sun Tran transit system, which is managed by the city of Tucson, Arizona.

That's a lot of governing structures! It's vital to make your demands of the right people. Tables 2.2, 2.3, and 2.4 are reference tools outlining the different branches of government and the powers they have regarding transportation issues.

Once you know what role you need to influence—like a mayor or a county supervisor—you can then check that governing body's website to see who is currently in that role. In this initial planning stage of

Table 2.2. Transportation-Related Powers of the Legislative Branch

General powers related to transportation	*Positions in the branch*	*Examples of their actions*
• Pass laws • Allocate and approve spending, including funding agencies and government programs • Empower and regulate agencies	Congress (Senate and House of Representatives)	Congress wrote and passed the American Recovery and Reinvestment Act of 2009.
	State legislatures	The Arkansas state legislature wrote and passed a bill that allowed cyclists to yield rather than stop at stop signs.[a]
	Board of county supervisors	The Hennepin County, Minnesota Board of Supervisors approved a multimillion-dollar grant to help build the Metro Blue Line Extension light-rail project.[b]
	City/town councils	The Oklahoma City Council approved a new bus rapid transit line.[c]

a. Joe Jacobs, "The Idaho Stop Becomes the Arkansas Stop," Arkansas Outside, September 2, 2022, https://arkansasoutside.com/the-idaho-stop-becomes-the-arkansas-stop.

b. Metropolitan Council, "Agreement with Hennepin County Will Fund Blue Line Extension Project Through 2024 and Establish New Governance Structure," news release, September 14, 2023, https://metrocouncil.org/News-Events/Transportation/Newsletters/Blue-Line-Extension-funding-agreement-2023.aspx.

c. Staff, "City Council Adopts MAPS 4 EMBARK Bus Rapid Transit Route," press release, Oklahoma City Free Press, July 8, 2024, https://freepressokc.com/press-release-city-council-adopts-maps-4-embark-bus-rapid-transit-route.

your campaign, once you figure out who you need to push, a lot of the rest of the campaign strategy flows from there. Fleshing out your plan takes learning more about your unique context, which the next chapter covers in detail. One thing to note, especially for first-time advocates, is that your campaigns will be heavily shaped by your political context. Depending on your political context, you might actually have an easier time winning change at a higher level of government than a lower level of government. For example, your city councilmember may personally

Table 2.3. Transportation-Related Powers of the Executive Branch

General powers related to transportation	*Positions in the branch*	*Examples of their actions*
• Appoint agency leadership • Direct agencies (within the confines of the law) • Enact policy • Sign bills into law or veto them • In the case of the president: manage foreign policy, which in turn has significant effects on the price of gas and other aspects of the economy	President	President Obama signed the American Recovery and Reinvestment Act, which provided over $15 billion in federal funds for transit, rail, and surface streets.[a]
	Governors	Arkansas Governor Asa Hutchinson signed a bill allowing "cyclists to slow down as they approach a stop sign and yield to right-of-way pedestrians and other traffic before moving through an intersection without stopping."[b]
	Mayors	Cheyenne, Wyoming Mayor Patrick Collins created the Cheyenne Passenger Rail Commission to "provide guidance and oversight for establishing passenger rail service in Cheyenne and serve as a local contact point for regional efforts."[c]

a. One Hundred Eleventh Congress of the United States of America, American Recovery and Reinvestment Act of 2009, 2009, https://www.govinfo.gov/content/pkg/BILLS-111hr1enr/pdf/BILLS-111hr1enr.pdf.

b. Tigist Layne, "California's Stop-As-Yield Law for Cyclists Has Safety Advocates Divided," The Coast News Group, August 24, 2021, https://thecoastnews.com/californias-stop-as-yield-law-for-cyclists-has-safety-advocates-divided.

c. City of Cheyenne, "Mayor Collins Announces Creation of Cheyenne Passenger Rail Commission," news release, December 11, 2023, https://www.cheyennecity.org/News-articles/Mayor-Collins-announces-creation-of-Cheyenne-Passenger-Rail-Commission.

hate transit, so getting them to approve funding for better bus shelters in your neighborhood would take moving heaven and earth. However, if your county is relatively pro-transit, you might have an easier time winning a pro-transit campaign targeting your county board of supervisors.

Shaping Your Dream to Your Situation

Now that you've gotten a stronger sense of what you want and how to generally aim your efforts, it's time to look at the broader context you are

Table 2.4. Powers of Transportation-Related Government Agencies

General powers related to transportation	*Types of government agencies*	*Examples of their responsibilities or actions*
• Enact laws • Create rules/regulations that clarify the letter and spirit of the law • Provide related services or contract them out to third parties • Allocate spending more specifically • Develop programs to help meet goals and directives	Federal Department of Transportation	In 2024, the US Department of Transportation's Federal Transit Administration updated its Public Transportation Safety Certification Training Program, which provides a uniform training curriculum and minimum requirements for rail transit and state safety personnel.[a]
	State Department of Transportation	In 2024, the South Carolina Department of Transportation published a new Statewide Rail Plan.[b]
	Local city departments responsible for roads, such as Departments of Public Works or Departments of Transportation (Note: A local Department of Transportation may also operate local transit service.)	The Sparks, Nevada Public Works Department is responsible for maintaining the streets in the city.
	Independent agencies that run transit operations, also known as transit agencies	The Greater Cleveland Regional Transit Authority runs transit service in the greater Cleveland, Ohio area.
	Metropolitan Planning Organizations (MPOs)	The Denver Regional Council of Governments produces the region's Coordinated Transit Plan to identify gaps between current transit services and needs and to examine how different projects might meet those needs.[c]

a. US Department of Transportation, "Biden-Harris Administration Finalizes National Regulation on Training Requirements to Improve Transit Safety Oversight," news release, August 14, 2024, https://www.transportation.gov/briefing-room/biden-harris-administration-finalizes-national-regulation-training-requirements.

b. *South Carolina Statewide Rail Plan* (South Carolina Department of Transportation, November 2024), https://www.scdot.org/travel/freight-rail.html.

c. Denver Regional Council of Governments, "Appendix J: 2050 Metro Vision Regional Transportation Plan Coordinated Transit Plan," https://drcog.org/sites/default/files/acc/TPO-RP-2050RTPAPPXJ-EN-ACC-24-05-16-V1.pdf.

operating in so you can hone your campaign plan and start approaching the general public about it. In learning more about your context, you may find all sorts of things that will help your campaign. For example, you may find that there are already other transportation advocates in your area you can link up with. The next chapter will help you localize your campaign plan and come up with points of connection so you are prepared when it comes time to start getting people on board with your vision.

Action Points

1) What is a transportation change you would like to see in your town, region, state, or country? What is a ***policy*** that your local, county, state, or federal representatives could pass that would make that change easier?
2) Figure out a rough estimate of how much it would cost to make your change happen. Search online to find comparable projects or reports from transportation experts that you can pull cost information from. **Bonus** How does that compare to the relevant sections of your city, county, state, or federal government's ***budget***?
3) What sorts of public events would help shift the local ***culture*** toward being more supportive of the change you seek?
4) When does your state, county, or city have to pass its next ***budget***? Look up the deadlines online and put them on your calendar.
5) Look up your local Metropolitan Planning Organization. What are they working on, and which items (if any) connect to the transportation change you would like to see?

CHAPTER 3

Understanding Your Context and Making Connections

Tailor advocacy efforts and reach specifically to [people] with issues that are very near and dear to their heart.—Deb Banks, Sacramento Area Bicycle Advocates[1]

Your advocacy exists within your unique contexts, which shape your ability to make the connections that will help you win. As Deb Banks, executive director of the Sacramento Area Bicycle Advocates in California's capital, put it, "I can go into a community and talk to them about bike lanes, and they can respond with, 'You know what, bike lanes sound great, but it's not my biggest need right now.'" In these conversations, community members might then list out a series of needs they find more pressing, like preventing dumping in their area, improving their sidewalks, or replacing their streetlights. When community members share about their context and needs, Banks points out that this is an opportunity to build a connection. She suggests replying with something along the lines of, "Let me put you on to some people that can help you with that," or "What can we do to help you get that so that you get what you need and are more ready to talk bike lanes?"

As Banks demonstrates, navigating your contexts can help you make connections with others. You'll need to connect with people because it takes more than one person to win a change for your community. When Banks and community members connect about how to meet the community's needs, they are also connecting on Banks's willingness to help the community. At a deeper level, they are connecting on the fact that the people in that community matter and their needs matter too.

Beyond helping you make connections with others, understanding your context can help you shape your advocacy so you have an easier time. For example, I'm aware that as a large white man, when I'm trying to talk to strangers and asking them to take a flyer or sign a petition, they may feel wary around me. I try to make up for that by being friendly, giving people a lot of personal space, speaking clearly, and being open to what they say in response to what I'm saying. Although I can never know someone's full context, I know that other people experience the world differently than I do, and I can have some humility about that. When a stranger ignores me when I'm passing out flyers and trying to talk with them about making our streets safer, I know it's not personal. To them, I'm just some guy on the street trying to get their attention.

On a macro scale, as transportation advocates, our context consists of all the transportation decisions and political fights that came before us. For example, our advocacy is shaped by our country's past and ongoing destructive, racist highway policies, as well as systemic disinvestment in our communities' capacity to build the transportation options we desire. We are also blessed by past victories from successful campaigns to make things better. Personally, I am so grateful that past advocates already won the fight to create my region's bus system. Not only does it make my life and my community better, but the fact that it's already here means I can focus my energies on other fights.

The first part of this chapter covers the political, cultural, and historical contexts we often have to contend with as transportation advocates. The second part of the chapter focuses on adapting your advocacy to your context so that you can build the connections needed to get the attention of decision-makers and win the transportation changes you seek.

Political Context

In order to make your vision reality, you need to navigate your political contexts to get decision-makers to agree to your demands. Chapter 2 covered who has which official powers to make the changes you seek, and that's just the tip of the iceberg of your political context. There is an entire ecosystem of political forces in your community; the decision-maker you are trying to sway is just one aspect of that.

For example, that decision-maker might be an appointee, in which case they may only be interested in taking an action that's approved by the person who appointed them. Or the decision-maker may be one of many people on a board, council, or legislative body who would need to approve your proposal. Additionally, there are likely specific details of the decision-making process—like a subcommittee that has to first review a proposal, or a specific time window for hearing proposals. Your political context can feel like an obstacle course your path to victory runs through. All it takes to slow your campaign's progress is a hurdle that you can't clear. Understanding your political context will help you navigate it.

Assessing and Mapping Out Your Political Context

To map out your political context, start with looking at who is officially in charge of the issue you care about and some basic information about them. Fortunately, some quick online searches or a chat with an experienced ally can turn up helpful information about this decision-maker. Later in this and the following chapters, we'll cover more about how to connect with allies, some of whom may already know a lot about your context.

To get a stronger sense of how your decision-maker fits into your overall political context, look up how they got into the position, their margin of victory if they were elected, and when they are up for re-election or when their term is up. As you flesh out your understanding of the decision-maker and their relationship with your overall political context, you will start to see how secure they are in their political power, which can affect how much and what sort of power you need to build in order to get noticed.

While every politician is unique, generally a politician with a tenuous hold on power is only open to doing things that gain them supporters without upsetting too many people. If they won their election by a slim margin, their political situation is less secure and they might not feel confident about their next election. When dealing with a decision-maker who's in a precarious position, you can win them over by showing them that you are a popular and organized potential ally. A politician facing a tough reelection may be looking for allies, and if they don't think it will come with much pushback, they may be willing to help you out. If you're asking them to do something that may make someone unhappy, show the politician that making you and all the people on your side happy will be more than worth the trouble.

Some politicians consistently win reelection with a wide margin and are secure in their power. They can be open to doing all sorts of things that aggravate some folks, as long as their main group of supporters stays happy. To win over politicians like these, transportation advocates can show that the politician's base is also on board with the proposed transportation change. For example, if you are trying to get a religious politician on board with your transportation proposal, try to get houses of worship, like the ones they attend, on board. Later on, this chapter and chapter 5 will cover how to make those sorts of connections. If you are asking for something small like a bike parking rack or a bus shelter and the politician's base of supporters doesn't care much either way, you can win—especially if the idea lines up with the politician's values.

Regardless of how secure the decision-maker may be in their power, no part of your political context is ever immutable. If a decision-maker's mind is unchangeable, sometimes the path forward means changing who the decision-maker is by campaigning to have them removed—if they were appointed—or to defeat them in the next election. We'll cover more about working with and against politicians in chapters 6 and 7.

Power Mapping

A common exercise for advocates looking to understand their political context and the context that surrounds their decision-maker is called power mapping. Remember: Although office holders might be the most visible parts of your political ecosystem, they are just one aspect of your political context. Power mapping helps you see the fuller picture.

In the words of the *Beautiful Trouble Toolbox*, a resource guide for grassroots activists, power mapping shows "who holds influence over [your decision-maker], and, therefore, who to target."[2] In other words, a politician listens to the people and groups that donated, volunteered, and otherwise supported their campaign. Those supporters helped make the politician's career, and they can hobble it too. There is a network of advocates, organizations, and coalitions that undergird the politician you want to move. If you can't move the politician directly, you can move them indirectly through that web of connections. If you need politician X to vote for your thing and politician X is beholden to group Y, getting group Y to tell politician X to support your thing will go a long way toward you winning.

Figure 3.1 illustrates a sample power map. In this hypothetical scenario, if you want to get the mayor to do something, consider trying to get the local business improvement district (BID) on board with the idea because they have influence over the mayor. If you have trouble getting the BID on board, you can reach out to local businesses directly to try to recruit them to the cause. They can reach out to the mayor themselves,

Figure 3.1. A sample power map. *Credit:* Fern K. Hahn

and they can influence the BID as they are members. Similarly, getting your neighbors on board helps the campaign by getting more people to reach out to the mayor directly, and it helps get neighborhood groups, who may also have influence over the mayor, to support your proposal.

Power mapping helps reveal the political context your campaign needs to navigate in order to get decision-makers to be *willing* to enact change. But their willingness doesn't mean they can actually implement your change. As transportation advocates, we must contend with an additional layer of constraints and possibilities that shapes our community's *ability* to enact change.

Political Context Shapes Technical Capacity

A government's technical capacity is its ability to actually follow through on people's demands. You might be able to get your city leaders to agree to build a bus rapid transit network, but if the city administration has never done such a thing, they likely don't have the capability to build it yet. In our interview, bike advocate and former Rochester, Minnesota City Councilmember Michael Wojcik explained, "When I got elected, I entered a system that was not interested, capable, or even prepared to make the bike-walk-roll changes we needed."[3] It took "a few election cycles to get new folks in there" and "a complete overhauling of the city administration" to get his city leaders *willing* and the city administration *able* to enact the transportation changes the community demanded.[4]

Rochester, Minnesota, isn't alone: Underinvestment in transit, bike, and street safety infrastructure is a countrywide issue and, unfortunately, a vicious cycle. Beth Osborne of Smart Growth America says, "You get good at what you do all the time . . . so [transit agencies] never get good at building [projects] because each agency is building so rarely."

We haven't gotten good at building transit infrastructure, and it shows when you compare what it costs us in comparison to what it costs our international peers. Transit projects cost 50 percent more to build in the United States than abroad.[5] Americans often lament our slow pace of high-speed rail development in comparison to China, and transit fans regularly point to the high-tech construction machinery used there, asking, "Why don't we have that here?"

The reason China can build high-speed rail projects faster, cheaper, and better than the US can is not because Chinese high-speed rail construction crews have an SL900/32 bridge girder erection machine that lifts, moves, and places entire sections of rail tracks while US crews don't.[6] Even if one of those machines suddenly appeared in Cincinnati, it wouldn't get put to work the next day to build a high-speed rail line to Indianapolis and Chicago or down to Louisville. Without the expertise and networks of resources that come from consistently building high-speed rail and getting good at it, that machine may not even get turned on. The more we build, the more we develop the mechanisms of training personnel, financing projects, acquiring land, getting permits, arranging material supply chains, and a slew of other resources that are needed to get good at high-speed rail.

Our inexperience, and the high cost of building that stems from it, can make it harder for politicians to support building transit—so we don't build. As transportation advocates we can break that cycle by getting our communities building and working to establish the ecosystem of policy, human capital, and technology that big transportation changes depend on. Technological capacity is not inherent to any one country or community. China developed its capacity to build high-speed rail. The same goes for Paris's recent bike infrastructure surge, and any other place's transportation development that one might envy.

Although our transit agencies and transportation departments have been starved for support for so long, they can still do a lot more than they are doing. Transportation justice advocate Haleema Bharoocha, who helps transit agencies and organizations across the country, emphasizes the importance of "focusing strategies on areas where agencies have control and the capacity to enact change." There are plenty of changes agencies can make happen at lightning speed; sometimes all it takes is a few signs and cones. We just have to remind them that they can do more and demand it of them.

For example, in 2020, the COVID-19 pandemic rocked the world, and it continues to disable and kill people to this day.[7] Many of our governments decided to take that threat seriously at first, and because keeping each other safe included keeping our distance, governments across America enacted "Slow Streets." With a few signs and temporary barriers, governments turned over street space from cars to people, making neighborhood roads safer for people to walk, bike, and socialize at a distance without fear of contagions or cars.[8] On a technical level, all it took was legal permission and some low-cost materials. While COVID-19 is still here and the Slow Streets programs brought benefits beyond reducing disease transmission, these programs have generally been dismantled, taking street space away from people and giving it to cars. There is no technical reason why every community in America couldn't recreate Slow Streets programs today. When advocates demand more from our government, we remind them that they have a lot of ability to make our lives better.

While American institutions may struggle with building transit, bike, and street safety infrastructure, our Departments of Transportation are often good at building highways. Pennsylvania rebuilt a collapsed section of I-95 in less than a week![9] While at first it might not be comforting to see how good our system is at building car-centric things, it is good to know that the government can build big things quickly when it's a top priority. Advocacy is a way to make an issue that is a priority for you into a priority for others.

When a decision-maker says they "can't" do something and not that they "won't" do it, you may have hit on a constraint that they are experiencing. In theory, once you fix that constraint, their "can't" disappears. Find a can't, fight to fix it, rinse, and repeat. In a sense, transportation advocacy is the work of demanding a change, then continually finding can'ts and resolving them until you win. To learn more about these "can'ts," you can ask more "why" and "what if" questions to the people in charge, such as "Why can we close the street to cars for a parade, but not for a street party?" and "What if we got you the money? What would the holdup be then?"

In your advocacy you may find hard technical limits to your victory, which could run the gamut from specific fire code regulations to a lack of specially trained staff. These limits are excellent issues for you to take aim at in one of your campaigns. In addition to these aspects of your political context, your advocacy needs to contend with a more fluid force and context: culture. Each community has a unique culture of its own, so it's helpful to refine your understanding of the cultural context you operate in and incorporate that into your advocacy.

Understanding and Adapting to Cultural Context

We exist in cultural contexts, which include what people will think of you, your idea, and your overall approach. As the removal of Slow Streets programs shows, sometimes cultural context is a bigger barrier than technical constraints. You can wage a fight to shift your cultural context with efforts like bike buses, transit parties, and other activities, as covered in chapter 2. You also likely need to adapt your advocacy to succeed in your cultural context. Understanding your culture is key to ensuring that your actions are read the way you intend, by the people you seek to organize and by the decision-makers you seek to sway.

Box 3.1 includes some questions to consider for a quick self-guided crash course in the cultural context you are operating in.

Mapping out your cultural context may involve listening to and growing your understanding of other people's different experiences of the world. That can vary across race, gender identity and presentation, sexual orientation, class, age, ability, religion, and more. You don't have to be a certain type of person in order to win a campaign, but it's helpful to understand how your and your allies' efforts may be received differently by your community or by decision-makers based on your different identities.

No matter who you are or where you are, you can be a successful transportation advocate. But you aren't campaigning in Anytown, USA, you are doing it in your unique community. You will have an easier time winning if you understand what's valued in your cultural context. As you better understand your culture, you can craft your approach to be more culturally resonant. For example, stories about bike successes

Box 3.1: Questions to Assess Your Cultural Context

- What is easy or common in your community? What is difficult or rare?
- What are people tired of? What are they excited about?
- Where, when, and why do people gather together?
- What are the visual cues that signal you are here versus elsewhere (colors, symbols, etc.)?
- What do different members of the community call the geographic areas your campaign focuses on? How you refer to an area and how you pronounce its name are some of the quickest ways you can signal to someone that you are or aren't from around there.
- Who do you think usually gets listened to or ignored in your community?

from Michigan or Minnesota resonate more strongly with people from Illinois than stories from California, explains Ride Illinois's David Simmons. "It feels more apples to apples," he says. When it comes to motivating Illinoisans to support pro-bike changes, he says, "it's good to look at our neighbors who are politically similar and highlight their example when they do something good."[10]

Similarly, you can better connect with a community when you align with its culture. When you dress and act the way your cultural context deems respectable, people can more readily absorb your message. Presenting the version of yourself that you and your audience are comfortable with is situational; sometimes that means formal wear, and other times that means a T-shirt and jeans is the appropriate attire. When in doubt, ask a friend.

Or you can craft something delightfully dissonant to stick out like a sore thumb. In a culture where "everyone drives," a bike brigade is sure to turn heads. Events like the World Naked Bike Ride, which had rides in hundreds of cities around the world in the 2010s, definitely get noticed.[11] Getting attention is easy: Do something big and out of the ordinary. However, as an activist you generally want *positive* attention that you can direct to your specific political goals. If you are trying to get attention by doing something out of the ordinary, aim to do something that will be celebrated, or at least accepted. Importantly, have a plan for how to make use of that attention once you get it; otherwise, you'll squander your moment in the spotlight. The purpose of the stunt is to get people to listen to you, so have something to say that moves your campaign forward.

Whether you decide to blend in or stick out with regard to your cultural context, look for events and news stories you can tie into in order to advance your issue. For example, transit agencies often make use of big cultural moments like concerts or sporting events to promote ridership, such as when Metro Transit in Minneapolis expanded service for the 2023 Taylor Swift Eras Tour.[12] As advocates, we have even more freedom to leverage cultural moments for our campaigns. For example, an advocacy group could set up a table near the transit stop at a music festival and collect petition signatures in support of expanding transit service. Even if some of the attendees are from outside the area, their desire for better transit to the venue still has weight—after all, better transit will help them spend more time and money in your area.

In addition to the cultural and political contexts of the moment, transportation advocacy also exists within a historical context, which still affects our communities today. You don't need to be a historian, but a richer understanding of your community's contexts will help you shape your outreach.

Understanding Historical Context

Part of assessing and mapping your current context involves understanding the historical context it came from. That can help you think about possibilities for changes you want to make and avoid repeating mistakes of the past. The harms of the past are often still very much in the present and can affect how open other individuals or groups may be to connecting with you on transportation issues. You may have come to transportation advocacy in the hopes of addressing some of those historic wrongs. Or you may be adapting your advocacy to your historical context, which often means opening your heart to the very real pain that surrounds our communities and the role transportation may have played in it.

Historically, large transportation infrastructure changes like highways or rail lines have significantly disrupted communities of color. This leads to justifiable skepticism from communities whenever advocates push for big new transportation changes. For example, in Minneapolis, Minnesota, the proposed Metro Blue Line extension goes through historically underserved communities, and many people were concerned that the extension would go hand in hand with rising rents and displacement.

As a staunch advocate for the project and for racial justice, Hennepin County Commissioner Irene Fernando works to prevent the project from repeating past harms. "Residents had long expressed concern about gentrification," she says. "Lots of transportation projects dismantle communities, so I, along with other elected leaders and transit planners, took the community's feedback on gentrification and concerns about being pushed out and rising costs."[13]

To address the concerns of Minneapolis residents, the coalition behind the Blue Line extension brought in other nearby cities and won $10 million from the federal government to fund anti-displacement efforts, such as preserving and building affordable housing near the rail line and making payments to help businesses hang on through the construction period.[14] In addition to avoiding gentrification, the project's proponents intend for the project to help heal inequities and better connect the region. With an understanding of the historical context, they are adapting their approach to mitigate harm.

The first step to address any problem is to recognize that it is real. In transportation advocacy, that often means listening to the people who have historically been hurt and who may be skeptical about new projects. The next step is to move beyond listening and put that feedback into tangible action in collaboration with the involved communities.

Historical context can impact support for your project because communities have long memories. Ground your transportation advocacy in your community's historical context and you can unlock all sorts of partnership opportunities that can help you win even bigger. Todd Scott of the Detroit Greenways Coalition explains that the planned Joe Louis Greenway is going through neighborhoods "that hadn't seen a planner in decades," so residents are skeptical of the project.[15] He says, "All of a sudden, the city is showing up to say, 'Hey, we want to build a biking trail through here.' Of course the community is going to say, 'Well, that's not for us.'" His group and community members worked with the city government to update the trail proposal so that it could address the community's historically ignored concerns. After that, the community members not only removed their opposition, they even became proponents of the trail.[16]

As the Joe Louis Greenway demonstrates, transportation advocacy is an excellent vehicle for righting past wrongs. By expanding your transportation advocacy to include those issues, you can help bring more allies to the cause. If instead you ignore your historical context, you may make potential allies wary of the solutions you are pushing. Many of America's problems are so deeply entrenched that if you aren't actively working to address them, you can easily end up making them worse. This frequently comes up in a range of transportation issues, especially matters of street safety and safety on transit, when some people propose carceral solutions such as police enforcement, surveillance, fines, and imprisonment.

The United States has a long history of relying heavily on policing to address traffic violations, and Ferguson, Missouri, exemplifies the shortcomings of that approach. According to a report from the

US Department of Justice, the Ferguson Police Department brought "roughly 24,000 traffic cases" to court in 2009 and over 53,000 cases in 2014.[17] In the small town of Ferguson, that amounts to roughly 2.5 citations per person in 2014 alone, yet even with that aggressive level of enforcement, a steady number of deaths from traffic violence still occurred each year.[18]

Traffic enforcement was not keeping Ferguson residents safe. Rather than a tool of safety, the Department of Justice report explained that traffic enforcement was explicitly used to systematically extract money from Ferguson's majority-Black residents to fund the city.[19] The yearslong systemic patterns of abuse at the hands of the police led to significant discontent among Ferguson's residents. When police officer Darren Wilson extrajudicially killed the teenager Michael Brown in Ferguson in 2014, community members rose up in protest.[20] The police department's militarized response drastically escalated the situation, provoking protests across the country.[21] Communities across the US have a painful history of police violence, which is deeply intertwined with our transportation system. Traffic stops make up 40 percent of interactions between police and adults in the US, and 10 percent of people killed by police were killed during a police traffic stop.[22] When advocating around these issues, it is vital that your advocacy be informed by this context.

To improve your advocacy and deepen your understanding of the intersections of transportation, race, and the US criminal legal system, the books *Inclusive Transportation: A Manifesto for Repairing Divided Communities* by Veronica Davis; *Cars and Jails: Freedom Dreams, Debt and Carcerality* by Julie Livingston and Andrew Ross; and *Arrested Mobility: Overcoming the Threat to Black Movement* by Charles T. Brown are excellent starting points.

While transportation issues have and can hurt communities, transportation advocacy can also be a path to healing our country, as demonstrated by the anti-displacement work around the Minneapolis-area

Blue Line. Transportation advocates can also address traffic violence and make biking, walking, and rolling safer for all while reducing abusive policing. The international organization Human Rights Watch has been focusing part of its work in the US on the nexus of cars, policing, and human rights abuses. Olivia Ensign, former senior advocate and researcher at the organization's US program, suggests that instead of policing, communities can create true safety for all by embracing safety measures like traffic calming, investments in community spaces, and other infrastructure-based changes. These, she says, will "begin to address historical imbalances; work toward better health outcomes; create navigable, sustainable, welcoming spaces; and decrease our reliance on surveillance and police for traffic enforcement."[23]

You might not have intended for your campaign for protected bike lanes or raised crosswalks to address more historical wrongs other than traffic violence, but it's wonderful that we can tackle multiple problems at the same time with the same set of tools.

While communities vary from one place to another, your historical, cultural, and political contexts are always there. They present challenges and opportunities when it comes to trying to make connections with others. From those connections, you can build relationships, and together you can build political power.

Connecting Your Issue to Other People's Priorities

Political organizing relies on connecting with others. While organizing boycotts of produce to improve conditions for farmworkers, the famous labor organizer César Chávez said, "The fight is never about grapes or lettuce. It's always about people."[24] As a transportation advocate, your fight isn't just about buses or speed bumps, it's about people: people's safety, people's quality of life, people's freedom to move. Viewing your advocacy through this lens will help you see the potential points of connection you can make with other people, such as potential campaign supporters, coalition partners, or even decision-makers.

Part of making that connection takes getting in front of those people, which can be done in person or remotely through social media, calls, or email. The League of American Bicyclists' Bill Nesper says that as the League, "We really show up in Congress with the National Bike Summit and with our daily presence on Capitol Hill wearing our bike pins," and "that consistent presence and relationship-building opens doors to policy conversations."[25] As Michael Kelley of Kansas City's BikeWalkKC puts it, "Elected officials are people just like you and me. If you understand their issues, and you know how to align your issue with theirs, you have everything you need."[26]

The easiest way to make a connection is by finding something you and the other person both care about. You already know what you care about, so next you need to know what the person you are trying to connect with cares about. Fortunately, as I've experienced firsthand across my years of advocacy on a range of topics, people care about a whole lot! People generally care a lot about what they consider to be "their" issues and spend a lot of time thinking about them—their to-do lists, their bills to pay, their passions. A big hurdle you face as a transportation advocate is that they are almost certainly not thinking about your particular issue. This can be distressing for advocates, but it's not personal and it doesn't come from a place of malice; it's just that people are busy with their stuff. You can get them to care about your thing by helping them see that it connects to their lives and interests.

There is always a connection between transportation issues and a person's top issue. As Pittsburghers for Public Transit's executive director Laura Chu Wiens explains, "Transit organizing really feels like it's at the heart of economic justice, environmental justice, racial justice, disability justice, and other efforts."[27]

For example, José Antonio Zayas Cabán, executive director of the Minnesota group Our Streets, often gives presentations to community members about highway removal. He always starts these conversations with the history of the neighborhood the highway destroyed, and the well-documented reasoning behind the government's decision to build the highway. When he lays out "the deliberate policies that segregated and harmed Black communities, it becomes clear that these highways weren't just infrastructure projects but tools of racial oppression."[28] Framing the conversation this way helps community members understand the importance of removing the highway. "By the time I'm talking about highway removal, the people want to burn that historic injustice down," says Zayas Cabán. He drives the point home in his presentations by asking: "Would you rather see this neighborhood restored and experience all of these benefits, or would you rather have five less minutes of driving time?"[29]

Beyond understanding your contexts, you can identify points of potential connection with others through a simple exercise. By asking yourself a series of questions and writing out the answers, you may unearth some building blocks of making a connection. Consider: What problem are you trying to solve? Why does it matter? How does your solution fix the problem? Who will the benefits impact? Who wins and who loses when this is solved? Table 3.1 highlights an example solution to a problem and takes a look at how that solution may benefit and impact others.

When asking, "Who wins if my desired transportation change goes into effect?" resist simple answers. It can be tempting to say "everyone wins," which is generally true when we have safer streets, greater mobility, and reduced emissions. But "everyone" is a big and vague concept, so it is not particularly useful for aiming your connection-building work. Throughout my advocacy, when I've tried to get people on board with something by saying it benefits everyone, people tend to say something

Table 3.1. Problems and Solutions Create Points of Connection and Potential Conflict

What problem do you want to solve? What is the solution?	*Who else wins with this solution?*	*Who loses with this solution?*
I don't want to have to wait so long for my bus, so I want more frequent bus service on the corridor near my house.	Everyone else who rides the bus Everyone who lives, works, or travels along the route who might ride the bus if it were more frequent Every business and destination along the route Drivers who would have fewer vehicles in front of them on the route People who appreciate cleaner air, safer roads, and lower carbon emissions from fewer cars	Car dealerships Maybe users of other bus routes if their route gets cut so that this route gets more service Maybe bus operators if the transit agency just pushes current operators harder rather than hiring more operators to run the service If your bus service increase requires reallocating funding that was going to be spent elsewhere, your change means someone else loses funding People who object to having more bus riders in the community, generally for bigoted reasons

like, "Okay, that's nice for everyone, but what about me? How does this help me?" To find points of connection between your issue and other people's priorities, look for complicated answers. Who are the different individuals and groups that make up "everyone," and how does this help them specifically? Here is where your understanding of your nuanced contexts will help you find even more potential connections.

Let's look at the California High-Speed Rail, which is the largest infrastructure project under construction in the United States today.[30] Completing the project requires more funding, and getting it that funding requires generating a great deal of political support. To connect the value of the project with voters and decision-makers, project supporters need to think creatively about who will benefit from the high-speed rail service. Contextualizing the project and getting specific will help show paths forward. For example, a typical Los Angeles resident might not care much about the ability to get to Fresno quickly and easily, but for the six thousand Angelenos who are Fresno State alumni, it's potentially a much bigger deal.[31] These alums could take the train to go to the big football game, the "Battle for the Valley," and see their beloved Fresno State Bulldogs take on their rival, the San José State Spartans.[32] There are likely a number of San José State alumni in LA who would be on that train with them!

Your campaign needs to build a lot of political power to win, and each connection you make is another piece of the puzzle. In the case above, winning over the LA chapters of the San José State and Fresno State alumni associations obviously would not build enough political power to win the billions in funding the high-speed rail project needs to finish construction. But they are a piece of the puzzle. Winning them over also helps when it comes time to win over another piece of the puzzle: LA politicians. A big advantage we have in transportation advocacy is that transportation changes make countless connections possible. Help people see themselves as direct beneficiaries of a change and they will become much more interested in it. As Bill Nesper of the League of American Bicyclists says, "[People] need to be able to see themselves in the story you are telling."[33]

Even if a potential ally might not directly benefit from the change you seek, you can still win them over. They might be interested in joining the cause if they see how your goal aligns with their overall values. For example, a merchant might think that their customers and staff don't take the bus and thus won't directly benefit from better bus stop amenities near their shop. However, they might agree that it is important to invest in the community and may support better bus stop amenities as a form of community enhancement. Or they might be sympathetic to people who need a place to sit while waiting for the bus, such as seniors. In terms of aligning with deeper values, your family and friends might not care about transportation issues, but they care about you and that could be enough of a hook to get them involved in your campaign.

Connecting with people who share your goals is essential to bringing them into your campaign and building your core crew of campaign leaders. The next chapter will cover how to build up a network of campaign supporters, volunteers, and leaders. Now that you have identified your potential points of connection and who you want to connect to, you are more prepared to try and make those connections. It's time to take action.

Action Points

1) **Power map:** Draft a power map by writing down: Who is the primary decision-maker you are going after? Who are the different organizations and individuals they listen to or are beholden to? Who are the people those organizations and individuals are responsive to?
2) **Cultural context:** Who are some respected members of your community? What do they value, what problems do they face, and how does transportation connect with them?
3) **Historical context:** Consider how the transportation change you want fits into the historical context of your area. Has it been tried before, and if so, what happened? Who would it affect, and what is their historical context in the community?
4) **Political context:** Look up the elected officials who represent you

from the local to federal level and look up their most recent election results. Write down their margin of victory in their most recent election in terms of raw votes and as a percentage of the registered voters in your community. You can likely find this information on the website of your local registrar of voters. Which of the politicians do you think is the most nervous about the next election and therefore might want to win over some new allies?

5) **Finding potential points of connection:** If you picked a campaign idea in chapter 2, consider what problem your idea solves. Write down a few sentences that depict how a person's life would be better if this idea were enacted. For example, "If this bus route had more bus shelters, people going to the mall, the senior center, and the high school would have an easier time waiting for the bus." Circle the places, people, or groups that show up in your story. These are potential points of connection.

CHAPTER 4

You Can't Win Alone, So Build Out a Team

Advocacy is a team sport. Nothing happens because of me; it happens because of we. An advocate's job gets easier when they're not the only person speaking up for that change.—Michael Kelley, BikeWalkKC[1]

Winning in politics takes convincing a lot of people to support your campaign and demonstrating that your desires are shared by others in your community. In her Minnesota district of about two hundred thousand people, County Commissioner Irene Fernando says, "If we get about a dozen constituents calling in about the same thing, then something is up in the district and our office needs to have an internal conversation about it." It's even more powerful when you get hundreds of constituents calling in about the same issue. Then, she says, "it's like, yikes, that's a big issue. Now we should do a coordinated response with the other county commissioners and coordinate with the county administration."[2] To flood a decision-maker's office with calls, you have to have a lot of people on your side.

One of the most important steps in a campaign is when your goal transforms from something you are pushing for by yourself to a shared vision you work toward with others. Campaigns are a huge amount of work, so you need more people to carry the load, especially if you are trying to take on multiple campaigns at once. Having more people involved improves the quality of your advocacy and helps your shared demands get taken more seriously. Ines Sigel of LINK Houston said, "No one can do this work on their own. It's too big. We need each other."[3] Fortunately, transportation advocates have a built-in advantage when looking for allies: There are lots of people who are already transit riders and workers, bike riders, and pedestrians!

As covered in the previous chapter, you have multiple ways to connect with people throughout your community. This chapter walks you through how to turn strangers into campaign supporters, volunteers, and co-leaders so that you can collectively do the work and build the power that's needed to win. You'll also learn how to work well with others and structure your collective workload effectively.

Getting People on Board and Involved

In activism there is a widely shared framework—the ladder of engagement—that outlines the process of turning strangers into supporters, volunteers, and leaders. The ladder starts with a low-effort and low-commitment action that a member of the general public can take to get on the initial "rung," as shown in figure 4.1. Higher rungs of the ladder correspond to increasing levels of engagement with the campaign or organization.

When a person takes their first step, like signing a petition, they get on the first rung of the ladder of engagement. The second rung is volunteering—taking a meaningful step to help move the campaign forward. A person can become a volunteer by doing something as simple as getting others to sign a petition. The third rung is leadership. Campaign leaders take initiative and ownership of projects or areas of work. For example, a leader could be the person who makes the petition in the first place, ensures that the petition gets translated into a different language,

Figure 4.1. A ladder of engagement. *Credit:* Fern K. Hahn

or crafts a strategy for bringing on more volunteers. Each rung of the ladder helps meet the needs of the campaign, and success requires getting lots of people on all of the rungs.

Kalli Krumpos of the Washington Area Bicyclist Association (WABA) explains how her organization gets people engaged by "meet[ing] our communities wherever they are in their journey around biking and offering resources."[4] She's often thinking about how to make it easier for people to move up WABA's ladder of engagement. "We acknowledge that sometimes we're making a bigger ask of a person to use some of their individual personal capital to go and meet with their policymaker," she says, so WABA tries to "make them feel supported and comfortable engaging in those more political conversations."[5] Moving up the ladder takes effort, so it's key to make each step as easy as possible. This is particularly important when it comes to initially connecting with people.

Turning Strangers into Supporters

Supporters are the people who are in favor of the campaign's goals and *do at least one thing to help bring about the change the campaign demands.* In chapter 3, we covered making a connection with potential supporters in a more theoretical way; now it's time to get into the details.

Before you approach a stranger, prepare a request or an "ask" of them. Having an ask is the difference between saying to a stranger, "Hi, I want bus transfers to be free," and asking them, "Will you sign this petition supporting free bus transfers, please?" A question invites a response and engagement. A good ask is something that is easy to understand and prompts action. An initial ask to sign a petition is a great way to give strangers an opportunity to become supporters; all they have to do is say yes and sign.

Your initial ask can also be an offer. For example, Sacramento Area Bicycle Advocates offers the community many services, such as pop-up bike repairs and bike valets. Executive director Deb Banks explains that those services are also "types of advocacy." Those services help get people riding, which shifts the culture. When providing those services, the group can also get more people involved because "we can talk to [people] about what's working and what's not working" about biking in the community.[6] A transportation advocacy group can also get people involved by cleverly filling in transit agencies' customer service gaps. For example, Atlanta-based transit advocacy group MARTA Army set up "a system where people could adopt a [bus] stop, print out real bus arrival schedules, and put [the schedules] up" at the bus stop.[7] Putting up these signs at bus stops helped people get more information about bus service, and the signs included ways for people to get involved with the advocacy group.

Once you create an initial ask or offering, you are ready to reach out to strangers. Start by reaching out to the people who would directly benefit from the change you seek. They are likely to form the backbone of the campaign. For street safety issues, look for people pushing strollers, people with young kids, people with disabilities, and seniors. As noted in the introduction, even people who are out partying can be potential allies; a great time to talk with them can be while they cross the street. For bike issues, look for people using their bikes to get around town and go to your local bike shop. To find potential supporters for a transit-related campaign, look for people using or trying to use transit. Don't forget the transit workers themselves.

As Laura Chu Wiens describes, Pittsburghers for Public Transit found supporters by "working with bus drivers to identify the biggest gaps in the system and hear their ideas around how service could be rerouted or reconfigured to serve those communities." As a next step, the group asked the bus operators about bus riders they had relationships with to "start to identify some of the riders who are leaders in those communities" and who might want to get involved.[8]

Finding Reluctance or Rejection

At the beginning of your campaign, focus on connecting with the people who do not need a lot of persuasion to get on board. Persuasion takes time and energy, two resources you are short on early in your campaign. If you knock on everyone's door on your street to see who else would support installing a speed bump, you will find plenty of supporters.

However, you might also find people who are uninterested. Those people might eventually be persuadable, so take note of what they have to say in case you want to come back later, but otherwise politely and quickly move on.

For example, one time I went from business to business to chat with each one about supporting a proposal to build a protected bike lane on the street. While many business owners gladly signed, a barber who was a self-described "avid cyclist" said he was fine with things the way they were since it was working for him. I pointed out that the protected lane isn't just to make it safer for people like him and me who are used to biking without protections from cars. The protected bike lane is needed so new people can get into biking without fear of traffic violence. He was unmoved. Since at that time the campaign needed businesses on board, but not every business nor that exact business, I politely wrapped things up and left to go talk to the next business on my list. Months later, when the campaign had more volunteers, a volunteer went back and had a lengthy conversation with the barber, eventually persuading him to support the project.

Sometimes you might encounter people who agree that things are bad but don't think it's worthwhile to try to fix them via political engagement. Abbey Seitz, director of transportation equity at Hawai'i Appleseed, explains, "If you feel like [the government is] not going to do anything no matter what happens, that's going to limit your advocacy."[9] People who feel that the system has never worked for them may be reluctant to engage with efforts to improve the system. However, if you help them see how the action you are asking them to take can realistically lead to the change you seek, you may be able to get them on board. Your enthusiasm may also be a bit contagious!

While some people may oppose your proposal, you will mainly find people who are too busy to care or take action. Getting politically engaged takes time and energy, which not everyone has. However, some people will be thrilled that you invited them to get involved. Many people are looking for opportunities to make a difference on things they care about, and some of them will be open to volunteering to help out the campaign.

Turning Supporters into Volunteers

When you need to do something for the campaign, ask supporters to volunteer to help. Volunteers are the people who answer the campaign's call for help with activities, such as making and passing out flyers, submitting letters to the editor of the local paper, putting on a campaign event, or anything else that helps the campaign. Chapter 7 covers volunteer activities in more detail.

Asking for Help

Depending on your past experiences with seeking help, asking for help might feel like a waste of time, uncomfortable, or even terrifying. But a wonderful thing about transportation advocacy is that a lot of people really want to help. As with trying to turn a stranger into a supporter, it is important to have a good ask when trying to turn a supporter into a volunteer. When crafting and making your ask of a potential volunteer, remember that volunteers can walk away whenever they want. Make it worthwhile for them to step up and take on more tasks.

Your ask should be something that is within their abilities, or something that they can reasonably grow into. My campaigns often involve flyering or tabling at events, and for those volunteers who are shy or hesitant to talk with strangers, I practice with them. I explain what tabling at an event is like and how it translates into the wins we're pushing for. When you are asking someone to volunteer, provide clarity about why the task matters and how it leads into the change the volunteer would like to see. If they say no, it is important to graciously accept their answer. Don't make it hard for them to say no; make it easy for them to say yes.

Make Volunteering Easy

In transportation advocacy, moving up the ladder of engagement from stranger to supporter to volunteer can happen quickly. Nearly every time I've flyered about a protected bike lane, at least one person is excited to find out about the campaign and asks, "How can I help?" In those instances, after getting their contact information, I hand them a small stack of the flyers to pass out. That may be all it takes to turn a stranger into a supporter and then into a volunteer.

When trying to get a person to spend their time volunteering, keep in mind that you are competing with everything else a person could spend their time doing, like watching TV or doing chores. Fortunately, you can make transportation advocacy a meaningful way to spend their time. You can also make it fun, like going for a group bike ride to pass out flyers or inviting people to help put together a party on the bus. You can also ask people what *they* would like to do. Being flexible about what volunteering looks like will help you get more volunteers.

Make it easy for people to bring their passions and skills to the campaign and they will. Transit advocate and Indianapolis City Councilmember Jesse Brown recalls a meeting when supporters of a bus rapid transit line were figuring out what skills they brought to the table. "We got people to step up and volunteer, with some people saying, 'I can do social media,' and 'Oh, I actually do graphic design for my day job.'"[10] Almost anything a person could contribute can be helpful in some way, but you may need to work with them to refine their idea. For example, if they want to do an interpretive dance to highlight the importance of transforming slip lanes into mini plazas, let them do it. Just make sure there is a big poster nearby with some explanatory text and a QR code people can scan to sign your petition.

Pittsburghers for Public Transit's Laura Chu Wiens explains that your role can be to help people direct their passion into advocacy. She says, "We want to be the vehicles in which people can move their anger and frustration into some existing process that we have . . . and show people how they can engage with [making change]."[11] When you ask someone for help, you invite them to move themself up the ladder of engagement. In doing so, you also move *yourself* up the ladder of engagement from being a transportation activist to a transportation "organizer."

As a reminder for the introverts who might be uncomfortable thinking about all this, *you* do not have to take the lead on the people-facing aspect of the campaign. You can lead on the parts of the campaign you are comfortable with, like making the campaign strategy or producing materials—as long as you empower other people to take the lead on other critical parts.

Empowering Volunteers to Become Leaders

In a campaign, there can be many different projects that all need leadership. A great thing about transportation advocacy is that anyone can become a leader. For example, in the hours building up to impromptu rallies I've led, people responded to my mass text invite with all sorts of questions, such as "Did you invite the media?" or "What should people's protest signs say?" To which I responded with things like: "I didn't, can you lead on that?" or "I trust your judgment on that, but if you're up for leading on it, can you please bring materials so people can make signs there?" Taking a step back from trying to do everything can create the space others need to step up into leadership. You don't have to know all the answers as long as you can encourage others to figure them out. Even if you are a budding transportation activist, you can mentor and train your groupmates, and learn from them too. Plenty of winning campaigns are led by a crew of people who are all figuring it out together as they go along.

Whether you pull people into leadership by nurturing their engagement or by creating a leadership vacuum, you should "invest them with authority and the trust to use it," as activist and author Starhawk writes in her book *The Empowerment Manual: A Guide for Collaborative Groups*.[12] Trusting in others' leadership requires accepting that people might make different choices than you would make. While you can share information in hopes that they will then reach the same conclusions as you, sharing leadership means giving up some control in exchange for getting more done. Fortunately, that trade-off is almost always worth it.

Working with Your Core Leadership Team

As volunteers step into leadership within your campaign, you will form a core team of leaders. These leaders are folks like you who want to expand the campaign in a certain direction and are willing to take on the responsibility of leading that work. As a transportation advocate struggling against car domination, it can feel amazing to be in a productive community with like-minded people who inspire and educate you. When advocacy is done in a collaborative environment it might not feel like work, but it still is. Make advocacy work as frictionless as you can by making gratitude, praise, and support abundant.

A positive environment is good in its own right, and it helps cushion the rough patches. Co-chair of the Rhode Island Transit Riders Patricia Raub explains, "We're all working toward the same goal, but sometimes we have strong arguments over the way a position paper should be written or what our next strategy should be."[13] Some tension is inevitable among your core team since you each have your own ideas and perspectives. When the Rhode Island Transit Riders "couldn't come to a complete consensus" on a particular issue, co-chair Amy Glidden explained that one member with a different position wrote an opinion piece "under their own name instead of our group."[14] Having different stances on an issue doesn't have to be a dealbreaker and doesn't stop everyone from continuing to work together on other matters.

Sometimes teams agree on goals but disagree on methods of getting there. This can be tough in charged moments like in the aftermath of a traffic violence death, when emotions are high and there is an urge to take action. In those moments, create space to work through it together as partners. People might have potentially conflicting fears: One person may be afraid that an action hasn't been fully thought through and can backfire, while another person might be worried about missing the moment by being overly cautious. Glidden suggests that advocates "embrace the hard conversation."[15] Opening up to each other can get more people on board and collectively plot a better path forward together. After all, advocacy is optional; if you try to bulldoze your allies and charge ahead on a course of action they disagree with, you will likely find yourself going it alone.

Agreement and Action

"Buy-in" is the combination of people agreeing on an idea and feeling invested enough to take action to support that idea. Make sure the decision-making process with your team generates buy-in so your collective decisions transform from words to deeds. For example, your group might decide it *should* pass out flyers on the bus, but if no one then volunteers *to actually pass out the flyers*, then the agreement isn't very useful. It's easy to agree that something is important to do, but harder to actually do it.

A key part of ensuring that you are generating buy-in is by consistently weaving the question of "who" into conversations. One way I like to do this is to bring half-formed plans to the group like, "I'm thinking of doing X, but I need Y to really make it work. If I commit to doing X, who is up for helping out by doing Y?" Proposing a half-formed course of action gives something people can react to while also inviting refinement. Stirring the pot can produce a range of reactions, such as "I will," "I would if you did it this way instead," and "What about ABC?" Asking if people are up for taking on a task can provoke a lot of idea-rich conversations, bring people into the group's decision-making process, and help them recognize that their role can involve helping refine the campaign's ideas and taking action.

Generating buy-in is essential because you're working with volunteers. Volunteering is completely based on consent, so if your fellow advocates don't want to do something, they won't. Laying out why the action matters and how it will lead to the desired outcomes can help generate some buy-in. For generating deeper levels of buy-in, it is helpful to have the decision come from a transparent process where people can share their perspectives and collectively decide what they want. If a person feels like they were part of the decision-making process for a plan, they generally feel more motivated to enact the plan.

Activist and author Starhawk says that in a healthy group, it is clear to all participants how decisions are made, how people can take on responsibilities if they choose to, and how people can get into decision-making positions within the group.[16] Transparent decision-making processes are part of a good organizational structure that supports your budding organization.

Structure

Organizational structures can help your group function better. Groups can build systems to do things like facilitating decision-making, welcoming new people, and establishing ground rules for how to treat each other. When a group is starting out, it is common for the default decision-making structure to be one where people choose to take on tasks and then are responsible for those tasks. In other words, everyone is their own boss or manager, and there's not much hierarchy. This structure is great for allowing people's passions to flow freely. It allows new people to join the group and immediately take on the tasks and leadership they want. This works well when people have a lot of initiative. Amy Glidden from Rhode Island Transit Riders explains, "I think a part of having a nonhierarchical structure is that it helps attract young people because they're not looking for all structure and process; they want to jump in and get to work."[17]

For some people, however, that kind of environment can be overly chaotic. An environment where roles and responsibilities are unclear, and the possibilities for ways to participate are endless, may produce paralysis or overwhelm people with options. Address this by making a more accessible welcoming process. That process can follow a highly structured model with orientation packets and presentations, or it can be more casual with greeters who welcome and situate newcomers.

Structures can also help your group navigate political and interpersonal disagreements. Shared group agreements can include aiming to understand one another and give each other the benefit of the doubt by trying to see things from others' perspectives. Starhawk offers a suggested norm: "We approach disagreements in the spirit of inquiry. What can we learn from this? What information might this conflict be telling us?"[18] Prioritizing curiosity can help soften conversations where people share values but are held back by their communication styles.

But not everyone means well. Oppressive attitudes in American culture permeate transportation advocacy spaces. tamika l. butler, former executive director of the Los Angeles County Bicycle Coalition and a national expert on the built environment and race, wrote: "My journey as a bike advocate has been full of ridicule, bullying, and harm because I—like many other advocates of color—dared to mention that safe streets should not be at the expense of Black lives."[19]

Unfortunately, transportation advocacy spaces can be just as racist, sexist, and bigoted as the broader culture. But you can make your campaign and organization a more welcoming place by clearly laying out your collective values and establishing a set of rules for group members to abide by. Many groups do this by establishing a group code of conduct. You do not have to recreate the wheel; look to other codes of conduct for inspiration. For example, Transbay Coalition, a San Francisco Bay

Area transportation advocacy group I co-founded, developed its code of conduct from several other organizations' codes. An excerpt states: "We take responsibility for our own participation and create space for the participation of others. We create a space that is welcoming for everyone regardless of ability, race, ethnicity, nationality, linguistic background, sexual or romantic orientation, gender identity, economic situation, age, or religion."[20]

While helpful, structures are just tools, and no set of rules can fix everything. You and your co-leaders will always have to manage interpersonal dynamics. Even among well-meaning people, conflict is inevitable, and your organizational structure will only be able to help so much. Similarly, your group's structures for decision-making or welcoming new members are only useful if people are able to use them to achieve their goals. Sometimes, organizational structures can even get in the way of the work. A classic example is when a quick decision is needed, but the decision-making process is structured so that the matter has to be referred to some committee that meets infrequently. Only establish structures you strictly need and get rid of structures that no longer serve your group. As your group expands and evolves, its structures should as well.

One way your group will likely evolve is by taking on multiple campaigns. When your group is structured to wage multiple campaigns at once, you can address more aspects of the transportation system, grow your group, and build up momentum.

Tackling Multiple Campaigns at Once

In transportation advocacy, we often need to push on multiple fronts to win. As chapter 2 explained, sometimes we need to win policy changes, budget changes, and culture changes all at once. Once you've formed a team of co-leaders, volunteers, and supporters, it is more possible to do that work. As the saying goes, "Many hands make light work."

When your group is deciding whether or not to take on additional campaigns, remember: You may get more people involved and unlock some efficiencies that come with scaling up your advocacy efforts, but the demands on your time and energy will also increase. Manage the workload and pick the right campaigns, and you will have a much smoother time waging multiple campaigns simultaneously. Standard tips for improving productivity in other aspects of your life also apply to advocacy.

Manage the Workload

Many of the same structures you set up for one campaign will help with future campaigns. For example, you can reach out to the email list of supporters you built from one campaign to ask them to support your other campaigns. A person who signed your petition demanding that your mayor put in speed bumps by schools would likely be interested in your effort to push for increasing state funds for traffic-calming improvements. Similarly, a volunteer who helped with graphic design for one campaign's flyer might be open to helping with a similar project for another campaign.

As your group's workload grows, the people who want to help also pile up. You and your co-leaders may become the bottleneck if you do not delegate. For example, if you are the only one who can make posts on your group's social media, you are the bottleneck to getting more content out there. Delegate, empower, and train volunteers so that the increased work can flow to multiple people and not just you and your original core leadership team.

You can take on more campaigns by developing more volunteers into leaders. Once someone has taken on leadership in the initial campaign, they are well-positioned to become a leader on a parallel effort. If someone has an idea for an additional campaign they want the group to take on, invite them to lead it. For example, if a person says, "The push for new bus route funding is great, but we should really work on getting more bus benches," you can respond by agreeing and delegating them as the leader of the new campaign to get more bus benches. You can also preemptively manage the workflow by picking the right campaigns to work on simultaneously.

Pick the Right Campaigns

Your group's decision to take on an additional campaign can be made suddenly to seize an opportunity, or you may make the decision strategically and carefully. Opportunistically taking on a secondary campaign can be as simple as supporting an eager volunteer to lead a new effort, or you may be responding to an unexpected threat or a new opening to win change. Your group will be well positioned to seize these opportunities if it has nimble decision-making structures and ensures regular movement up the ladder of engagement.

When taking a more strategic or long-term look at which additional campaigns to wage, consider what your initial campaign needs. If you want to bring more allies into the fold, taking on additional campaigns gives people more opportunities to plug in with your group. Courtney Jackson, executive director of Ride New Orleans, explained in our interview that "a business might come [to us] because they want to talk about regional rail, and we'll talk to them about that, but we're also going to talk with them about funding the local bus."[21] By campaigning for multiple things, Ride New Orleans can bring in supporters who may have initially just been interested in one of the campaigns but can learn to value the other campaigns too. Pulling people in on one campaign and then guiding them into your other efforts is especially helpful if you're having a hard time getting people excited about a particular campaign, as depicted in figure 4.2.

Your campaign may be having trouble getting people excited if it's at a slow point in the process. For example, if the decision date is far off,

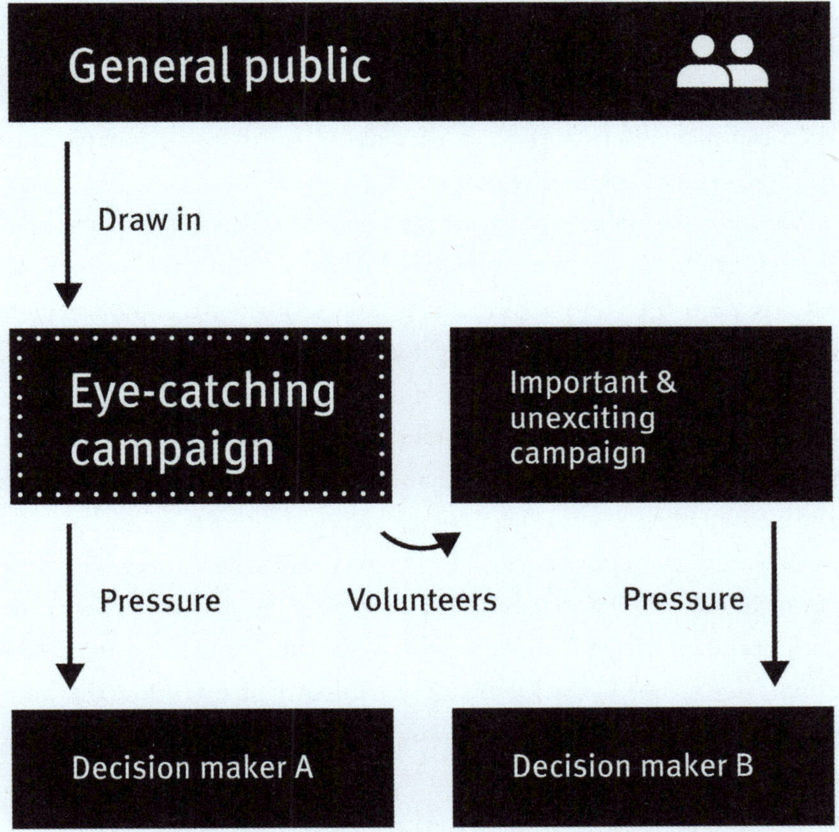

Figure 4.2. Waging multiple campaigns can help get more people involved. *Credit:* Fern K. Hahn

the campaign may lack a sense of urgency. In these instances, you may want to pick up an additional campaign that is moving on a faster timetable. Transportation campaigns in particular can progress slowly, which runs the risk of volunteers losing interest. Engaging in multiple efforts at once helps keep the energy up and keep your advocacy top of mind for supporters, the general public, media, and decision-makers. With multiple ongoing efforts, your group is always doing something, and thus you always have an opportunity to engage with people. Reporters and politicians have countless other issues to think about, like housing, healthcare, and their own lives. Generally, if they aren't actively working on transportation issues, they aren't thinking about them. But you can keep transportation issues on their radar by consistently having campaigns that demand their attention.

You can also evaluate potential campaigns by their type and consider the synergies that could be unlocked by taking them on. For example, a cultural effort to get more seniors on transit in your community pairs nicely with an infrastructure campaign to get better bus stop amenities, and either of these pairs well with a campaign to get more funding for transit service. A unified theme along different types of efforts is naturally reinforcing, making it easier for campaign leaders to collaborate and pool resources.

Bike advocacy groups generally do this very effectively. Many host "learn to ride" clinics that get more people biking, thereby shifting the culture and growing their membership list. At the same time, many bike groups advocate for specific bike infrastructure changes and the budgets to enable them. These efforts build on each other, target different decision-makers, and help keep a steady cadence of activity to pull more people in.

Ensuring Campaigns Don't Trip Over Each Other

A downside of waging multiple campaigns is that sometimes the campaigns can get in the way of one another. You can have only one highest priority of a decision-maker or a reporter at a time, so ensure that your campaigns are targeting different decision-makers. When evaluating potential campaign combinations, pay special attention to pivotal dates when you can expect either campaign's decision-maker to make their decision. For example, a legislative campaign's schedule will be dominated by the calendar and processes of the legislature. Meanwhile, your local government's budget-making process has its own schedule. If those budgets are set at roughly the same time, working on both might be too overwhelming. But if their schedules line up so you could have one campaign in a sprint while the other has a bit of a lull, that might be perfect for your group.

In terms of topics, if your campaigns have demands that are *linked* but have separate decision-makers or timelines, the campaigns are unlikely to get in each other's way as they can function like one big campaign with two connected demands. For example, a campaign to get a state agency to study a particular rail corridor for upgrading service and a campaign to get the state legislature to pass a policy removing hurdles to rail corridor upgrades are not going to conflict—and will likely support each other. Inversely, when you pick campaigns that are totally *distinct* and have different decision-makers, the efforts are unlikely to come into conflict.

Ultimately, the best way to ensure that your group can successfully take on multiple campaigns at once is to build power. The bigger, stronger, and more capable your group is, the more it can do.

Building Power

When you build out a campaign filled with supporters, volunteers, and leaders, you collectively build power. That helps you win and take on additional efforts. In addition to people power, what you strengthen in one campaign—like material resources, legitimacy, and knowledge—can carry over to another. For example, if you build a website to support your freeway removal campaign, it is relatively easy to add a section on your website for your secondary campaign. Other resources needed in one campaign—like poster-making supplies, donations, and organizational structures—can also be used for other efforts.

While a less-tangible resource, your legitimacy can also build through experience and can translate across your campaigns. Legitimacy is the weight your words are given because you are the one who said them. If you are viewed as a legitimate voice on transit during a policy campaign, you will be viewed similarly on a budget campaign regarding transit. With more legitimacy, more decision-makers are likely to take you seriously, as will reporters and potential supporters.

Similar to your legitimacy, knowledge is a type of power that will help you across your campaigns. Activism and campaigning are learnable skills: When you study them (as you're doing right now) and put them into practice, you will get better. Each campaign you wage will teach you lessons you can apply to improve your other campaigns.

The network of connections you have built is another powerful resource that grows with each campaign and carries across all your efforts. When Ride New Orleans made business contacts who were interested in the group's rail advocacy, it laid the groundwork for working with those businesses on another campaign. Remember: You are not alone in wanting the change you are advocating for, and your group isn't alone either. There is a wide world of organizations that may be open to collaborating so you can all win bigger victories together. Much like how you as an individual are stronger when you form up with others in a group, your group is stronger when it works in coalition with other groups. The next chapter is dedicated to coalitions, which can be powerful changemakers.

Action Points

1) Consider your campaign goal and think of a specific, simple, direct ask that a person could say yes to in order to move the issue forward.
2) Ask a friend to help you practice making that ask. Have them pretend to be a stranger and together role play different scenarios where they respond to your ask by saying "no," "maybe, tell me more," "yes, what else can I do to help?" or by totally ignoring you.
3) Reflect on how that went. What went well? What could be improved? Incorporate those improvements and try again. The more

you practice your asks and getting different responses to them, the more you get used to it.

4) Look at which groups already work on transportation issues in your community. See what their priorities are and decide whether you want to propose your idea to them. **Bonus** If you feel ready and think that they could be aligned, reach out to them. If they don't want to take that on as a project, it could make sense to start your own group. You can still stay connected with that other group, perhaps as part of a coalition. Chapter 5 lays out how to connect with other groups and work in coalition in more detail.
5) Write down a list of people in your community you could approach about a campaign idea. Reach out and ask if they would be interested in talking about a potential campaign. If you can't think of anyone to start with, take your sample ask out into the community and strike up conversations with strangers.

CHAPTER 5

Win Bigger in Coalition

Working in coalition with other organizations helps us all score the changes our community needs.—Eric Rogers, BikeWalkKC[1]

The Kansas City–based advocacy group BikeWalkKC regularly works with schools to make it easier for students to walk and bike in their neighborhoods, and that work often introduces the group to other organizations in the community. Executive director Eric Rogers recalls how after seeing BikeWalkKC's successful partnerships with local schools, refugee resettlement groups "would come to us saying, 'Transportation is the number one challenge for the clients my organization supports.'" The refugee resettlement groups explained to BikeWalkKC how when new Americans miss the bus or if their car breaks down, "they miss their shift at work so they lose their jobs, so they lose their housing, so they lose custody of their kids."[2] With the understanding that transportation problems connect to their target issues, refugee groups and other organizations started working in coalition with BikeWalkKC toward collective victories.

A coalition is a "temporary alliance of distinct parties, persons, or states for joint action," and together groups are stronger than they would be on their own.[3] This chapter will help you understand how coalitions can make your campaign smarter, stronger, and more capable of a wider array of activities. This chapter also covers how to build a coalition by identifying potential coalition partners and getting them on board, as well as how to work together to win your shared goal.

Advantages of Coalitions

Forming and working in coalitions is vital for winning big transportation changes. By joining with other organizations, we have a better chance of getting decision-makers to take our demands seriously. "Rail advocates demand rail funding" is not worthy of a newspaper headline, and it's easier for a decision-maker to tune that out because of course that's what rail advocates want. But when "the businesspeople" or "the justice people" are joining "the rail people" to demand train improvements, that makes the demand seem more reasonable and can make potential opposition seem fringe.

For example, in 2024, when an Iowa bike advocacy group led the effort for a crosswalk improvement law, they focused their messaging on how the legislation would help non-cyclists, such as senior citizens. Next, the group's executive director Luke Hoffman explains, "We intentionally built out our coalition with stakeholders from our messaging, including AARP Iowa." The AARP (formerly the American Association of Retired Persons) is one of the most politically engaged and largest organizations in America: Roughly one in ten Americans is a member.[4] AARP Iowa "registered in support of the bill and sent out action alerts to their membership at a key moment."[5] In the end, the crosswalk bill passed unanimously in the Iowa Senate and with a huge margin in the Iowa House, 84–8. By bringing more groups into the campaign, the bike group had a better chance of winning.

Coalitions Expand What a Campaign Can Do

Coalition partners can work in parallel and distinct ways, which can collectively strengthen the whole campaign. This can be helpful because not every campaign tactic is available to every group for various reasons. For example, one group might have a large donor who would pull funding if the group did something too radical. When you have a variety of groups in your coalition, you may unlock a diversity of tactics the overall coalition can take.

Let's revisit the 2023 campaign to save transit in California, as mentioned in the introduction. California transit agencies were facing a financial crisis that was going to result in huge cuts to service. On top of that crisis, California Governor Gavin Newsom proposed *cutting* transit funding by billions of dollars.[6] Transit supporters did not take that lying down, and advocates of all stripes used the tools they had to push for change. For some, that meant blocking a freeway as part of a piece of street theater protest. For other groups, that meant using the direct lobbying access they had to the governor's office to try and negotiate a deal. At no point did the rabble-rousers in the streets and the lobbyists in the capitol link arms to block the freeway, nor were they both at the negotiating table with the governor's office. But the groups were in a loosely coordinated coalition when they *independently* took the actions that only their group could; chapter 6 covers that strategy in detail. By using a variety of tactics, the overall coalition was able to exert significantly more pressure on the governor, and we not only got him to reverse his proposed cuts, but also to add over a billion dollars in new funding for transit.[7]

Coalitions Get More People Involved

When coalition partners activate their networks to take concrete actions, like calling their elected representatives or going to a protest, a lot more people will get involved—which is more likely to sway decision-makers.

Coalition partners can also help get the campaign's message out to more types of communities. Your coalition partners will have different cultural contexts and competencies than you, so they can help craft the campaign's messaging and approach to resonate with their community. In addition to helping with messaging, your coalition partners might also be better messengers to a community because they have preexisting relationships or are more capable of establishing trust.

If some community partners or residents are not yet very open to what you have to say, Hawai'i Appleseed's director of transportation equity Abbey Seitz recommends, "Work with people who are actually trusted by the community and are already working with them."[8] One way her organization put that into practice was by collaborating with trusted community health workers to do community engagement on a campaign about transportation issues faced predominantly by women and caretakers in a multiethnic and underserved area.[9]

Working with partners who aren't transportation experts also helps remind us to use words everyone can understand. When transportation advocates are overly accustomed to talking among ourselves, we can forget that phrases that may pique our interest, like closing slip lanes and installing bollards, might not mean anything to most people because they are highly specialized terms.

Coalition Partners Can Help Refine Your Goal

A core question transportation advocacy tries to answer is, "How can we make our transportation system work for more people?" Fortunately, coalition partners have much to teach transportation advocates about how to answer that question. This is in large part because everyone has different experiences and needs when it comes to making use of our transportation system. Partner organizations can bring in the expertise of their community's lived experiences and help you come up with a better solution to fight for.

For example, people have different transportation experiences depending on whether they use a mobility device or not. The width, slope, and condition of a sidewalk might not matter much to a person who is currently able-bodied, much less to someone in a car. But for someone who uses a cane, a wheelchair, or a stroller, those barriers to mobility can seriously disrupt their day. Anna Zivarts of Disability Rights Washington explains, "You're never going to be able to anticipate these access needs in the way that someone who experiences them day in and day out will know them."[10]

Making our transportation system more accommodating can involve any number of things, like getting public restrooms at transit centers, level-boarding ramps for buses, and wayfinding signs that are legible to people who are color-blind. Keep in mind, your initial "ideal" solutions might have some unexpected issues. "The solution you're seeking . . . may actively create barriers for people with different access needs," says Zivarts.[11] Coalition partners with different lived experiences are invaluable resources for helping shape what to campaign for so you can make more people's lives better.

Transportation justice advocate Haleema Bharoocha explains, "Centering lived experiences is essential to crafting policies that truly meet community needs." This principle guided her work on the Bay Area Rapid Transit (BART) "Not One More Girl" campaign, which brought together young people, community-based advocates, and artists to address sexual harassment on public transit.[12] Roughly five hundred Bay Area girls and gender-expansive youth contributed to the project through narrative-driven art, which educated fellow riders on how to disrupt sexual harassment when they see it. The project also involved coalition member–led research that informed policy fixes, such as the BART board passing a prohibition against sexual harassment. This may seem like an obvious improvement to make, but this explicit prohibition is rare among US transit agencies. A survey of results from the first phase of the campaign showed a 36 percent improvement in people feeling safer on the transit system.[13] This progress was only possible because advocates brought in and elevated people with different lived experiences than the people the agency typically heard from.[14]

Each coalition partner brings their own insight and abilities to the table, so the more diverse your coalition is, the more skills your campaign can access. One of those skill sets your coalition partners might bring to the table is political experience. Partners who are experienced changemakers may have insight regarding the campaign's political context and the strategy and actions that may be needed to win. For example, a partner can share intelligence that they are privy to, like the kind of messaging that will resonate with the decision-maker. Similarly, a coalition partner with technical expertise on the transportation issue in question can help the coalition understand the problems and proposed solutions from that angle.

Coalition Partners Can Share Resources

Beyond their people and expertise, coalition partners each bring additional resources to a campaign. A school might have a gymnasium you can use for an event, an artist might have access to sign-making materials you can use for a rally, and if your coalition partner is a business or cultural institution with a physical location, they can help show support and bring in more supporters by hosting an event or putting up a sign. This is particularly helpful when you are campaigning for an infrastructure change, as it shows that the idea is popular in the proposed area.

To facilitate the sharing of materials—like audio/visual equipment or a printer for the campaign—ask and you may receive. Keep in mind that the people you are working with in coalitions might not know the full inventory of things their group could lend. Feel free to ask them to check with their team about materials. They might not know that their group has access to a podium, a folding table, or other useful items for the campaign.

Figure 5.1. The Atlanta group Beltline Rail Now advocates for a light-rail line along the Atlanta Beltline and provides window stickers for businesses along the Beltline who support the proposal. *Credit:* Matthew Rao

In addition to material resources, partners can bring connections they can potentially share with the coalition. When working with a community that wants a streetlight, Deb Banks of Sacramento Area Bicycle Advocates would help them by saying, "I'm not the streetlight people, but I might know who is."[15] Then she would make the introduction, sit in a couple of meetings, and bow out. Sometimes all someone really needs is to be put in touch with the right person. A coalition member can also help connect their partners with other groups, government officials, reporters, and more.

Things get a bit trickier when it comes to sharing money in a coalition. In transportation advocacy, there is never enough money. That scarcity can lead to organizations being guarded or even prickly about the topic. However, a group's pocketbook tends to open a bit more if the money being requested is earmarked for some specific vital campaign activity your group can do that their group could not do. For example, a group with deep-pocketed donors may not want to engage in disruptive activities themselves, but they are well positioned to funnel resources to rowdier grassroots groups that are rich in passion and could do something eye-catching for the campaign if they had the financial resources.

Given that a coalition would be an asset to your campaign, let's talk through the nuts and bolts of building one! The first step to forming a coalition is figuring out who to invite.

Identifying Potential Coalition Partners

Identifying potential partners uses the same connection-building skills as discussed in chapter 3: Start by thinking through who might benefit from your hoped-for transportation change. From there, consider which sorts of organizations or companies might be interested in those people. For Ride New Orleans's Courtney Jackson, in her city, that includes "certain interests, like the hospitality industry, or major employers, who know that a big part of their workforce gets to work riding the bus."[16] These industries and employers recognize that transit is essential for getting workers to their jobs and so they are open to working in coalition on some pro-bus issues.

When it is time to identify specific potential allies, search online, read through relevant media, and ask around in your community for recommendations. If your campaign is focused on a specific geographic area, like a neighborhood or a street, Google Maps is an amazing resource to find nearby entities. You can also take your search offline by taking a walk around the area to see which organizations or groups operate there.

Another way to identify potential allies is to power map, as discussed in chapter 3, which looks at which groups are close with the decision-maker you are targeting. Bringing a decision-maker's key ally into the campaign is a surefire way to get your demand noticed. If the decision-maker you're focused on is an elected official, look up their major political donors on websites like OpenSecrets.org, or check their campaign website to see which groups have endorsed them.

While there are many great organizations to partner with, be aware of organizations that want to use transportation issues to divide, criminalize, or impoverish communities. There are also organizations that claim to be pro-transit but anti–wasteful spending, and they may be interested in partnering with you on a transit agency accountability effort. But if these groups only critique transit projects and never highways, they may use you to hurt transit.

But most of the time, any group who wants to join your coalition is an asset, and the most likely snag you will encounter is that there isn't enough time in the day to reach out to all the potential partners you would like to. Prioritization is key.

Prioritizing Your Outreach

Start by reaching out to groups that are already primed to jump in and help out. Natural allies who often engage on transportation issues will not need much convincing to get on board. Depending on the issue you are working on, that may be environmentalists, urbanists, senior and disability justice groups, neighborhood associations, or economic and racial justice groups. It may also include other transportation groups that work at the local, regional, or national level.

Once these low-hanging fruits are brought on board, think through what your group and partners bring to the coalition and what is missing from the winning equation. For example, if the changes you're campaigning for could be viewed as disruptive or radical, focus your outreach on bringing in allies who are viewed as mainstream or "normal." Getting a local house of worship, a community leader, or a community institution aligned with your cause will make it harder for the decision-maker to brush off the campaign's demands as unserious. When Hood River, Oregon activist Megan Ramey (from chapter 2) was starting out, she said she was "known as the 'crazy bike lady' in town" until her daughter's elementary school principal collaborated with her "to organize a bike parade during COVID distance learning."[17] If the local elementary school principal is on your side, how fringe or radical could you really be?

Relatedly, focus on recruiting coalition partners who can blunt possible opposition to your proposal. For example, a common reaction to street safety measures is concern about hurting nearby businesses. Beth Osborne of Smart Growth America points out that "it helps to have a bunch of business leaders in that area on your side ready to say, '[This street safety improvement] won't hurt the economy; it'll be great for my business. It will help me attract talent to work in this location and help bring in customers.'"[18]

Once you've built out your list of potential partners and prioritized who to reach out to, it's time to start your outreach.

Recruiting Coalition Partners

The coalition recruitment process is fairly straightforward: Introduce yourself and have a conversation. Tell the potential partner about the problem you are trying to solve, explain how it relates to them, then invite them to join up! Of course, there are some nuances to keep in mind.

How you approach a potential coalition partner may vary depending on how you want to work with them. If you're aiming for something quick and shallow, and if your group already drafted a letter with your demands to the decision-maker, then you can ask potential partners to sign on to it. Letters like these are known as "coalition sign-on letters," and chapter 7 will discuss how to write one. If a group agrees to sign on to the letter, add them to it and thank them. You can follow up to see if they're interested in taking additional actions, like sharing a petition with their network or participating in a campaign event. When you are seeking a long-term relationship with a group, invite them to have a larger conversation with you about their needs and priorities as it relates to the overall topic you want to collaborate on. While preparing for and during that conversation, you can learn about their priorities and see where your interests overlap. This may feel familiar because connecting with a potential coalition partner takes similar skills as connecting with individuals, as covered in chapter 4.

To bring partners on board, Bakari Height emphasizes the importance of giving them something they need. In addition to being the cofounder of the advocacy group MARTA Army, he is also the transit equity organizer at the nationwide group Labor Network for Sustainability, where part of his work entails working in coalitions with unions to advance transit and housing in Maryland. He said in our interview, "Maryland has 105 passenger rail stations. That's 105 opportunities for housing." Working to get more housing built near transit is "a win for the building trades, a win for the electrical trades, and a win for the transit unions; that's a win for a lot of organizations."[19] Think about how your issue can help your potential coalition partner accomplish their priorities, and center your outreach on that.

Throughout your outreach, you may find that some groups don't want to work with you. They might flat out disagree with you, not see what's in it for them, or just be too busy to engage. But you don't know until you ask. When I was working to build out a coalition for a local bike lane, I didn't think the furniture store would sign on, but it turns out they were thrilled about the idea because the store owners bike to work and the furniture store ships directly to customers from the factory. You don't know what the local gun range owner, farm bureau, or tattoo parlor will think about your transportation goal until you actually talk with them about it.

If your initial outreach to a potential partner happens over email and they do not respond, check back in a week or so with an updated message. If another week or so passes and you still don't get a response, try changing up your approach by calling, going to talk to them in person, or changing your messenger. For example, you could have a mutual connection reach out. Just remember that these potential partners don't owe you anything, and you are the one asking for their help. If they respond with a request for more information or ask tough questions, that is a good sign. Engage with them in good faith as you would an individual volunteer, which we discussed in chapters 3 and 4.

When you are having a hard time bringing an ally into your coalition, put yourself in their shoes. Ask yourself, "If I were them, why would I care?" For years, I fielded these questions at my job in the solar industry where I worked to get busy business leaders engaged in a political struggle that was difficult to understand. I had to address valid questions like, "What's in it for me?" and "Why should I care?" all the time. Taking those questions seriously usually means looking for deeper answers than "It will save lives," "You'll make money," or "It is the right thing to do." It can be frustrating if those answers aren't enough, but it's important to move beyond frustration so you can work with more people and get more done. Michael Wojcik of the Bicycle Alliance of Minnesota said he wished he had "spent more time coalition building than being angry" when starting out in advocacy.[20] "It held me back. . . . I got more done in the later years once I focused more on coalition building and building support behind the scenes."[21] Getting frustrated with potential partners doesn't help you bring them on board; deepening your empathy and understanding of their situation is a better pathway.

If a potential coalition partner does not want to engage even after you've made it clear how they would benefit from a particular transportation change, there are likely other factors at play that you have yet to consider. One factor is that politically powerful entities aren't sitting around waiting for you to come pitch them on your idea; they've got their own plans. For example, when I asked to join a local labor council's meeting to pitch them on supporting a campaign for electrifying the regional rail line, I was a five-minute agenda item on a full day's docket. Generally, organizations are already busy, and your campaign might not be worth their time. Relatedly, a group that understands how they will benefit from your campaign may not want to get involved if they have an ask of that same decision-maker on a separate matter that is a higher priority for their group. For example, if you are campaigning to get the mayor to build more sidewalks, a union preparing to renegotiate contracts with the city might want to save their energy for their own campaign rather than deploy their resources to help with your campaign.

Fundamentally, campaigning is work, and when you invite a group to join a campaign, you are asking busy people to put in work they hadn't anticipated. To address this, make your campaign more worth their time and attention, generally by catering your demands more to that group's needs. Another option is to ask them to do something that is easier or takes less commitment than whatever your initial ask was. If they don't want to publicly sign on to a letter, maybe they will attend an event where they can learn more about the issue, or allow you to give a short presentation to their group.

Another thing to keep in mind is that powerful potential allies might be petty. In an extreme case of this, Laura Chu Wiens of Pittsburghers for Public Transit explained that her "county's transit agency staff were told [by the county executive] for years that they'd be fired if they talked to us."[22] If you are in a situation where it seems like everything lines up but a potential political ally *still* isn't getting involved in your effort, it's possible that they might have some petty grievance holding them back. Or they might be so dead set against a perceived opponent that they don't mind if the problem persists as long as it means their perceived opponent doesn't get a win.

If would-be allies are refusing to work with you, don't waste your time courting them. However, handle those situations gracefully because it is the right thing to do and it also keeps the door open for future collaborations. Move on and build up the coalition without them. Pittsburghers for Public Transit have won plenty in spite of that county executive's refusal to work with them, and their situation eventually shifted anyway as the county executive later switched jobs. Don't dwell on the negative; you have plenty of other potential allies to bring on board, and you can win a lot with them!

Once you've formed a coalition, then it is helpful to figure out how you want to work together.

Coalition Styles

Coalitions can work together in all sorts of ways. From my experience working in various coalitions and talking with other transportation activists, coalitions' internal setups fall anywhere along a wide spectrum. On one end of the spectrum, you can do what I refer to as "cooking" up a coalition. These coalitions can be relatively unstructured, where you opportunistically recruit partners as you campaign. On the other end of the spectrum, there is what I consider to be a "baking" coalition, where you first bring all the groups together and collaboratively decide what to work on and how you all want to go about it. Let's take a closer look.

Cooking Up a Coalition

When you have your heart set on a specific issue, like getting a new bus-only lane on a corridor, and want to get organizations on board, then an approach that's more on the "cooking" end of the spectrum is helpful. In this style of coalition formation, you take your fleshed-out campaign idea, invite a bunch of different groups to join in, and the group of organizations that agree with the idea end up forming the coalition. I think of it as a cooking style since you are essentially putting whatever ingredients you can get into the campaign, stirring things up, and seeing what happens. It's a useful style for when you want a wide range of potential groups to join the campaign—such as the businesses along a corridor—and to do it quickly.

In these loose coalitions, members will have a wide range of engagement levels, from doing the bare minimum to co-leading the campaign. Members of these coalitions function more as decentralized cells or a "hub and spoke" model, in which partners do not need to participate in coordination meetings or even work with each other, as long as each one has a connection to the central node of the coalition. As the likely hub of the coalition, your group's role is to work with those who join up and make it easier for them to take action to advance the campaign. Courtney Jackson of Ride New Orleans says, "The more work that we do to make it as easy as possible for people, give people talking points, put the work in their hands . . . it's very effective at getting them to engage."[23] If you are asking your coalition partner to email their members an action alert about your campaign, send the partner a complete email draft so all they have to do is copy, paste, and send it out, as mentioned in table 5.1. You may also want to provide sample social media posts they could use in addition to the flyer, image, or link you want them to share.

Unlike the "ladder of engagement" (covered in chapter 4) for getting individuals more involved in campaigns, coalition partners take a different approach when it comes to deciding which actions to take. Each partner is unique in terms of what interests them and what is easy or hard for them to do. So, offer them a buffet of actions and encourage them to fill their plate however they want. At a minimum, a coalition partner just needs to agree on the goal of the coalition and do something helpful toward achieving it. Sometimes that helpful thing is simply a public affirmation of their support of the coalition, like when they let you list them as a coalition member.

In these "cooking" style coalitions, groups can act more independently to move fast and do a lot. While a "cooking" coalition style takes little commitment from each partner and can produce solid results, coalitions that follow more of a "baking" style can be powerful in other ways.

Table 5.1. Making It Easier for Your Coalition Partner to Boost the Campaign

Ways a coalition partner can boost the campaign	*How to encourage it*
Publicly endorse coalition's demands	Send them the coalition sign-on letter; ask if they want to sign on. If they say yes, add their logo, name, and the name of the person signing on behalf of their group to the letter.
Spread the message to their network	Create campaign-related sample emails and social media posts. Share these with the partner and ask them to use these resources to spread the word. Ask if your group can present to their network at an event or join in at one of their upcoming events.
Speak with media	Offer to introduce them to reporters and quote them in campaign press releases.
Direct outreach to decision-maker	Give them talking points about the campaign and information on how to contact the decision-maker. Invite them to your lobby meetings with the decision-maker or their staff.

Baking a Coalition

A "baking" coalition style typically focuses on building group cohesion, which helps the coalition function as a large, united front. I think of this coalition style as similar to baking because groups are thoughtfully brought together in specific ways to form into a cohesive entity. In these styles of coalitions, members may find it worthwhile to invest in collaboratively crafting shared visions and internal processes. Investing that energy into the inner workings of the coalition can pay off when the groups are in it for the long haul and will want to work with each other again and again.

An example of a coalition that invests in the ties between its members is the SacMoves Coalition, which is based in and near California's capital city. Starting in the late 2010s, the coalition has collaborated on a range of issues at the nexus of transportation, housing, and air quality.[24] One way the coalition members deepened their engagement and got more in sync was by building a framework of shared values they are all committed to. Sacramento Area Bicycle Advocates (SABA) is a member of the coalition. SABA's executive director, Deb Banks, explains, "The lung people [the group Breathe California Sacramento Region] can see themselves in [the shared framework], and the housing folks can see where they fit into this larger set of value statements about SacMoves" as well.[25] Building deep alignment and commitment to working closely together helps build the trust and systems that are needed for all these different groups to act as a cohesive unit over the long term. It is incredibly powerful when a variety of groups—like "the lung people," "the housing folks," and "the bike people"—join up, unite behind a single demand, and speak in one voice to a decision-maker.

For coalitions on the baking end of the style spectrum, this focus on discussing values and goals among all the different members can sometimes mean the coalition ends up spending more time talking than taking action. Talking is a key part of the process to get to coordinated action, but at some point that collective action needs to happen. Getting on the same page and talking should be in service to that end.

Your coalitions will likely fall somewhere between these two extremes of pre-planning and making it up as you go along. In the end, the gold standard for a coalition is one where the partners are comfortable working together and play to their strengths while dedicated to the overall mission.

Navigating Coalition Dynamics

Working in coalition with other groups comes with a set of dynamics similar to those you might encounter when working within your own group, which chapter 4 covered. Being up-front with one another about potential differences—such as differences in interests, temperaments, and priorities—can make it easier to intentionally deal with those differences. For example, I have worked in coalition with a group that essentially refused to engage with a particular politician, even though I collaborate with that politician's office regularly. That group has always been clear about that boundary, so it has been easy for me to respect their stance. The respect goes both ways: I've been clear with my coalition partner about why I will continue to work with that politician, and they accept that about me. Sometimes navigating differences with coalition partners can be easy when you can just agree to disagree about something, and instead you can all focus the coalition's energies on making progress on what you do agree on.

However, some disagreements cannot be ignored and can threaten to fracture a coalition. Laura Chu Wiens suggests addressing such disagreements by having an open conversation, getting to the root causes, and figuring out the shared core problem.[26]

Often, tension can arise when coalition members fight over some artificially scarce resource when the real answer lies elsewhere. For example, bus operators who have to keep to a tight service schedule can have tensions with bus riders whose boarding-time needs aren't accounted for in that schedule. If bus operators feel pressured to stick to a strict schedule, they may pass people up at transit stops, fail to take the time to properly secure people's wheelchairs onboard, or not wait for people to be settled in before driving off. A bus operator who takes the time to help riders can improve safety and rider satisfaction but may end up having to try to make up for lost time by skipping their own break time, speeding, or risking being penalized by management for falling behind schedule.

Laura Chu Wiens has dealt with these tensions in coalitions that include bus riders and operators. She has worked with riders and operators to help them "understand that the reason the bus is behind is not because of the person with disabilities [who may need more support or take a bit more time to get secured safely on the bus] or the bus drivers" who may be crunched for time. The real issue is "that the schedules management made are unrealistic."[27] One of her solutions is having coalition partners work together to get transit agency managers to build more time into the bus schedules so operators have the time they need for their breaks and the time they need to help people get on the bus and settle in. It may take a bit more effort, but getting to the root cause of an issue can expand the conversation so all coalition members can understand each other's perspectives and identify solutions that work for everyone. Winning those solutions often means uniting to go after a larger goal. Embracing our coalition's diversity also helps develop a richer understanding of the problems we seek to solve.

Another common point of tension within coalitions is when partners have different strategic understandings or disagree on whether a particular action or message would be effective. What appeals to one partner may not work for another partner. Coalition partners will view things differently because of their varying identities and experiences, which shape their understanding of how things work. The framework for this concept, which comes from feminist and queer theory, is called "positionality."[28] For example, your and your partners' positionalities may mean you disagree about how important it is to organize a rally for the campaign or how much work it takes to make that happen. If a coalition partner finds organizing rallies to be difficult and ineffective while another believes they are useful and easy to put together, the coalition's discussion on whether or not to hold a campaign rally might be tense.

However, differences in positionality among coalition partners can be a strength for the campaign as long as partners respect those differences and coordinate the campaign efforts to make those differences assets. The earlier example of the effort to save California transit service from the governor's proposed cuts was in large part successful because the "respectable" nonprofit groups and the "rabble-rousers" in the streets each took actions aligned with their strengths while loosely collaborating. Had the partners demanded that the entire coalition join them in their specific action, the alliance likely would have fallen apart.

Things to Avoid While Working in Coalition

The main pitfalls when working in coalition are relatively easy to avoid: misrepresentation, failure to follow through on promises, and poor communication about transportation issues.

- When speaking with the press, decision-makers, or the public, be very clear when you are speaking on behalf of the coalition versus when you are speaking on behalf of your group or yourself as an individual. When you gain access to a decision-maker on behalf of the coalition, use it for your coalition, not for your individual group.
- Don't promise coalition partners things you can't guarantee. Do what you say you are going to do, and if it turns out you won't be able to follow through on something, let your partners know and together try to figure out a new plan.
- Communicate in an accessible way about transportation issues with your coalition partners. It's unrealistic to assume that all coalition partners have the same knowledge and expertise. As a transportation advocate who spends time reading books like this one, you may be familiar with more specialized language and case studies about transportation issues than your coalition partners who focus on other issues. Share what you know.

Coalitions Are Greater than the Sum of Their Parts

Collectively, a coalition can orchestrate its efforts for maximum impact by leveraging each coalition member's strengths. The next chapter will focus on how to do that using a powerful and proven campaign strategy.

Action Points

1) If you are part of a group, create a list of your organization's strengths and weaknesses, which can show you the gaps a coalition partner could help fill.
2) Create a big list of different *potential* coalition partners in your area. Note why you would want them on your side (or at least not opposing you), and how *they* would benefit from getting engaged with the campaign.
3) Highlight the potential partners you might expect to work with multiple times on different campaigns.
4) Reach out to those potential partners. Introduce yourself and your campaign to get the ball rolling on building a coalition!

CHAPTER 6

Deploying an Inside/ Outside Strategy

By having good relationships, being a trusted partner, and by representing a big group of grassroots advocates from around the country, we're invited to the meetings [with decision-makers], and when we get in we push, push, push, but also work in partnership.—Bill Nesper, League of American Bicyclists[1]

One way to pressure people who have official power to meet your demands is to stand outside their offices and shout. You can also get heard when you have a direct conversation with those people or their staffers, sometimes literally inside their offices, which is also known as lobbying. So far, we've covered strengthening your campaign's ability to get heard from the outside by bringing in campaign supporters, volunteers, leaders, and coalition partners. However, there is a whole other front where you can sway decision-makers: from the inside. When a person has access to a decision-maker, that "insider" is positioned to persuade the decision-maker and shape their decisions. Bringing a transportation idea into reality often takes pushing from the outside and the inside at the same time. The strategy of coordinating the two fronts is referred to as an "inside/outside strategy" or "working the inside game and outside game."

This chapter explains how to gain and leverage access to decision-makers and agency staff to play the "inside game." It also covers how you can become an influential insider or collaborate with "insider" groups that already have a lot of access. In addition, the chapter explains how to use an "inside/outside strategy" and outlines how transportation professionals can be active inside allies while operating within the requirements of their official roles. First, let's take a look at the participants of the inside game, how it works, and its limitations.

The Inside Game

How much of an insider you are depends on how much influence you have on the decision-making process. For example, as a member of the general public, you are usually on the outside, but on issues affecting your street and neighborhood, you are closer to the inside than people who live elsewhere. Likewise, if you are a constituent of a county supervisor, you will get a friendlier response from them when you reach out to schedule a meeting compared to someone who doesn't live in their district. If you make a personal connection to your town councilmember or their staff—from having volunteered on their campaign or through your regular engagement on local issues—you have even more inside connections. If you work for a transit agency, you know a lot about how that transit agency works.

There are a lot of access points to the inside on transportation issues because these issues touch communities in so many ways. Everyone involved with the decision-making process—including elected officials, agency staffers, committee members, and community stakeholders—is a person you can work with to shape the final outcome more toward your liking. You can also become one of those insiders through your outside advocacy. Bill Nesper explains, "As an outside activist, when you get to a certain amount of power, you get to a point where you have to be in that [decision negotiation] meeting, where [the decision-maker] invites you to be in that meeting . . . all of a sudden, you're on the inside now."[2] Whether you start out on the inside or end up working your way there from the outside, you will work on the inside with elected officials, government agencies, or special committees that each have their own abilities and needs.

Working Directly with Elected Officials and Their Offices

Depending on the campaign you are working on and how you navigate your context, you might identify an elected official who wants to collaborate, potentially by introducing a bill. If the elected officials in your area are initially unmotivated to work with you, they may be swayed by the network of supporters and coalition members your campaign builds. But getting an elected official on your side is just one step. They will face barriers to implementing the transportation changes you want; you and your allies can help them overcome these hurdles.

A common hurdle is that it takes a lot of work to shepherd a proposal through complicated official government processes. Elected officials usually have their own priorities they are trying to enact, and their staff often have overflowing workloads already. Even their own priorities can get pushed to the side. According to Beth Osborne of Smart Growth America, "[Elected officials] walk into the office with a list of things [they] hope to do and they quickly get lost by all the incoming stuff," such as demands from constituents and other duties of the office.[3]

Grow the capacity of their office by providing an extra set of helping hands. Help them do the work needed to take your transportation demand through the official decision-making process. Osborne recommends asking elected officials and their staff questions like, "How can I support you? Do you need my help in drafting [policy]? Is there someone I should be working with to support that drafting? . . . Do you need me to go get [legislative] co-sponsors? If so, what kind of co-sponsor do you need?"[4] This is common territory for advocacy groups that play the inside game. Collaborating with an elected official's office often involves helping them do their job.

A key power many elected officials have is to write policies. Get the ball rolling by translating your idea into a written policy. Some advocacy groups specialize in this type of inside work, such as the conservative American Legislative Exchange Council (ALEC) and its liberal counterpart State Innovation Exchange (SIX). These "policy shops" draft legislation language and put it into the hands of eager elected officials. With the drafted legislation in hand, a lawmaker is then freed up to work on the other steps needed to pass the bill. Transportation-related policy shops are rare, but our movement does have some, like the San Francisco Bay Area Planning and Urban Research Association (SPUR). While organizations with policy expertise have their own agendas they are pursuing, their websites can be a treasure trove of reports, data, and policy briefs you could pull from to support your campaigns.

Drafting policies is easier than you might think. Osborne explains, "Just put something down that everyone can react to. . . . You shouldn't twist yourself in knots to get things perfect because it's a starting point and it's going to change a hundred times before it takes the next step."[5] Even if you have never drafted policy before, you can do it. The first time I drafted a policy was when I collaborated with then-assemblymember Rob Bonta (now California attorney general). I responded to his invitation to constituents to submit policy ideas and proposed a bus-only lane on the bridge connecting San Francisco with the East Bay. After he replied positively, I wrote a policy brief on the issue to help others get up to speed quickly. The brief detailed the problem, who it impacted, how the solution would address the problem, and how to implement the solution.

From there, the policy experts at SPUR joined the cause—as it aligned deeply with their policy priorities—and did the heavy lifting, working with the assemblymember's staff to translate the concept into official bill language. That inside work was an essential part of moving the bill to the next stage of the process. With that taken care of, I had more time to focus on the outside game work of getting local support for the proposal. In short, Assemblymember Rob Bonta granted us access, and we were able to bring in the extra helpers, policy expertise, and political will needed to move the idea forward.

Another stumbling block that might prevent a politician from embracing your idea is their concern that your proposal could negatively impact people they care about. If you have direct inside access to a politician or their staff, they may tell you who they want you to bring on board before the politician is comfortable taking more steps. Address this by working with the people or groups an elected official is concerned about. If a politician tells you that they are open to your idea but want to hear what the local businesses think, then go talk with the local businesses about it. You may find that they don't have a problem with your idea; if so, relay that message to the politician—or better yet, have them tell the politician directly. If they do have concerns, hear them out and see how you can win them over. That may take adjusting your proposal.

When our coalition fought for that bus-only lane, our partners with inside access to representatives from the state highway agency spoke with them to hear their concerns. The negotiations resulted in the agency removing its opposition in exchange for us changing the proposed bill. Rather than requiring the agency to create a bus-only lane, the bill would require them to collaborate with other relevant agencies to ensure that bus travel times through the corridor met certain high standards. The agency thought they could do that without a bus lane, and if they could, great. If the agency's plan didn't work, then they would almost certainly have to install a bus lane anyway. Because lawmakers often defer to the experts at government agencies on technical matters, opposition from an agency can sink a proposed change. Our inside allies did essential work by facilitating conversations and figuring out which specific changes were possible.

Another major hurdle is that sometimes a politician's concern is about the impact on their own career. They might not want to pursue your idea out of fear of the political repercussions they might face. The change that makes you happy may anger other constituents or entities with a "special interest" in the issue, like business associations, unions, or other advocacy groups. In these situations, give politicians "political cover" by making it clear that the politician would be politically safe if they did what you are asking them to do and showing that you have more people, coalition partners, and energy on your side. Building up your outside game also shows politicians that your side is the one they should be afraid of making unhappy. This is an example of how inside/outside coordination strengthens your advocacy, which we'll cover more later in this chapter.

Lastly, a willing decision-maker is not all powerful and might lack the votes needed to pass the bill. Their colleagues' lack of support can stem from all the same things we just covered, as well as a lack of demand from *their* constituents. In these cases, consider expanding your outside game organizing work—including your coalition outreach—into the districts whose representatives you need on your side.

Working with Government Agencies

Depending on the campaign you are working on, you will need to deal with different actors, including government agencies, as covered in chapter 2. In theory, these agencies are politically neutral implementers of the policies passed by elected officials. In reality, the people at government agencies have their own ideas of how things should go and can tip the scales accordingly. If they support a proposal, they can choose to go above and beyond in their work on the topic. Or if they oppose a change they have been tasked with working on, they can do the bare minimum, delay it, or let it "slip through the cracks."

For example, in 2023, the town of Burlingame, California, cut a two-day car-free block party short after complaints and confusion.[6] The mayor said, "We didn't coordinate with the public or the merchants well enough and we didn't promote it well enough to be successful."[7] Somewhere within the inner workings of Burlingame's city administration and agencies involved with the project, the staffers responsible for doing that coordination and promotion dropped the ball. To put the project planning on the right track, advocates pushing for the block party could have used inside allies to spot this issue ahead of time and alert outside allies, who could then pick up the slack by doing that coordination and promotion work. We'll revisit this example in more depth later.

If you are an agency staffer, you have many ways to tip the scales toward the outcomes you want without having to rely on outside game connections. One way is through contextualizing issues to subtly sway the decision-makers you report to. This can happen, for example, when agencies need to report on how many parking spots would be eliminated for a street safety project. Let's say that installing a protected bike lane would require removing thirty parking spaces. A staffer responsible for creating that memo could make that number of parking spaces seem small by presenting it as a percentage of the total spaces on that stretch of road. They could shrink the concept of thirty spaces even further by sharing it as a percentage of parking spots within a reasonable walking distance. If they want to push the envelope and make thirty parking spaces feel like nothing, they could frame it as removing thirty spaces to save a certain number of lives each year. All of these are accurate ways to talk about the project, and each one shapes how decision-makers feel.

Another opportunity for staffers to use contextualization to tip the scales comes when they need to report on community feedback they have received about a proposal. If a staffer supports a proposal and they receive lots of community feedback against it, they can provide context for that response by comparing the total number of individuals who spoke out—and perhaps their demographic information—with the entire community, the vast majority of whom likely didn't weigh in at all. This can help decision-makers see that those who spoke out against the proposal are a small and nonrepresentative sample of the whole community.

While advocates tend to spend a lot of attention on elected officials, agency staff also have a lot of power. If you are an outside advocate, play the inside game by bringing a relentlessly positive and problem-solving attitude to conversations with agency staff. Keep in mind, these internal allies at transit agencies or Departments of Transportation are often pushing against the status quo of their organizational culture. Even if we have elected officials and some agency staff on our side, institutional inertia can still foil our plans. If your plans are stuck within an agency, strengthen your campaign's outside game while continuing to evolve the sophistication of your inside game.

Advocating Inside Official Committees

Another component of government processes is the "committee," where appointees review transportation matters that are under consideration by a governing body. Committees are often made up of community members and other stakeholders who are brought in to be part of the official decision-making process. You might consider pressuring one of those committees or even becoming a committee member, but first, see if it's worth your time by considering the actual level of influence the committee in question has. If a committee exists to produce reports or give feedback on staff reports that help frame matters to decision-makers and the community, that committee can be a channel for getting your group's perspective heard. A committee may also be given the responsibility to review all proposals before they go on to the city council, in which case the committee may have the power to kill, stall, or advance a project. That is some real power, so committees like these are important arenas to engage in.

Do not lose sight of the fact that committee members are frequently appointed and empowered by elected decision-makers, such as mayors or councilmembers. That elected official may also have the legal authority to revoke or subvert the committee's powers, replace a member on a whim, or even just ignore the committee entirely. Sometimes, a committee is just a sideshow or even a distraction—elected officials still have the real power. If you decide to advocate at the committee level, make sure to still push the ultimate decision-maker as well. Your specific situation will vary, so look into a committee's powers and limitations to see where it may fit into your advocacy efforts. You can learn a lot by attending a committee meeting or chatting with a friendly committee member.

The Possibilities and Limits of the Inside Game

In transportation advocacy, there is a lot of space on the inside, so it is easy for transportation advocates to overly focus on the inside game. To be fair, the inside game can win drastic change without outside game support. Let's revisit a story from earlier that typifies an inside game victory. Chapter 2 mentioned that Ride Illinois won a new state road standard that created miles of bikeable shoulder lanes. Through their long-running advocacy work and relationship-building efforts, the group built connections with the Illinois Department of Transportation (IDOT) and developed expertise in dealing with the agency. Around 2005, IDOT was going through an internal process to determine the standard place on state roads to mark the shoulders. Ride Illinois caught wind of this and realized that if they could get IDOT to standardize the installation of painted lines and rumble strips on the far left of the shoulder, bicyclists would have more road space. Ride Illinois marshaled inside coalition partners that worked on IDOT issues, and collectively, they presented their case to the agency, eventually getting IDOT to agree to the new pro-bike standard.[8]

This exemplifies inside-game efforts in several ways. First, the campaign depended on inside knowledge and access: Only someone with a sharp eye on the department would even know this process was happening. Second, spotting this opportunity required an appreciation of how details translate into real-world improvements. Third, Ride Illinois and their coalition partners were able to successfully navigate official processes to get their proposal considered. Fourth, the victory makes a meaningful difference in the lives of a lot of people, but it does so in a way that might not be flashy and doesn't lend itself to outside-game efforts. "Left-side shoulder striping NOW" is hardly the rallying cry at a passionate street protest. All of this combined highlights the silent power of the inside game: It can profoundly shape our world while staying under the radar.

However, there is a fifth element of the story that reveals the limits of an inside-only effort. If IDOT decided to ignore Ride Illinois, the bike group would have little recourse. Saying no to Ride Illinois wouldn't cost anyone at IDOT their job, nor would IDOT lose funding. The advocates won because they were right *and* their input was valued. If they were right but dismissed by IDOT, they would have lost. Outside advocacy helps loudly amplify the demands of inside advocates, putting more pressure on decision-makers. By bringing a large number of people into the conversation, outside advocates can intensify the threat (or promise) of political consequences for a decision-maker based on their decision. That can go a long way in inspiring decision-makers to make the decisions we want them to make.

Inside/Outside Strategy

The individuals and groups working on the outside and inside need each other. Without the outsiders, the insiders may lack the raw power they need to get their points taken seriously. Without the insiders, the outsiders' message may be left out of the negotiation process. Deploying an inside/outside strategy is the work of coordinating allies across these different positions to collectively achieve something they couldn't win independently. The inside/outside game works in three common ways: bringing the outside in, bringing the inside out, and what I think of as being "independent together" (to borrow a term from the artist Rebecca Sugar).[9]

Bringing the Outside In

At certain moments, decision-makers are particularly open to hearing what the community has to say on transportation issues. Inside advocates can identify these openings—like a committee hearing or when the matter is coming to a vote—and flag the situation to their outside allies. Outside allies can evaluate the opportunity and decide whether it's worth mobilizing their base of supporters for that moment. If you've ever received an email with an "action alert" like calling your representative about an upcoming vote, you have been downstream of this effort to bring the outside in.

Another common way to bring the outside in is by sharing reports and stories from the outside with decision-makers. Statistics and studies are helpful tools of persuasion, but nothing beats having a constituent sit down with an elected official to talk about how the transportation issue affects their life. Groups with inside access can set up lobby meetings in which outsiders bring constituents who can speak passionately about what the law would mean for their community. Bringing that visceral understanding of the issue from the outside to a direct meeting with the decision-maker is powerful. When trying to persuade a politician or their staff, remember the tips from chapter 3 about making connections based on shared values. Michael Kelley of BikeWalkKC explains, "A person saying, 'I really want a crosswalk here because it would make it easier to take my daughter to the park' is more meaningful than ten people repeating the same stat about crosswalk safety when they see the councilmember."[10]

In addition to setting up the lobby meetings, insiders can prepare their outside allies by translating the proposal from technical language into terms a layperson will understand and care about. During the lobby meeting, people with inside access can help by steering the conversation to keep it productive and focused on the actions that are within the decision-maker's power.

For new activists, lobby meetings can be intimidating, but in Kelley's experience, "99.9 percent of the time, elected officials don't get mean; they don't want to create bad publicity." He warns that a vague answer from a decision-maker can be the worst outcome from a meeting: "'I'll look into this further' is sometimes worse than 'No' because you may end up chasing a 'No' you could've gotten in the first place." To turn a noncommittal maybe into something you can work with, Kelley advises, "Be prepared to push for something firmer."[11] If you can't get a good sense of where a politician stands on your issue during the meeting, consider asking them something about your topic that is easy to say yes to. For example, invite them to take a transit ride with you and fellow constituents. How they respond will give you a lot more information about them.

Bringing the Inside Out

While lobby meetings traditionally take place in the official halls of government, we can also have our meetings in the places we are trying to bring attention to. Being able to literally point to the issue we want a politician to solve is a huge advantage we have as transportation activists because it helps us make our demands memorable. Bring the decision-maker out into the community so they can experience the issue firsthand. For example, if you are talking about transit service, invite them to ride the bus with you, which will give you ample time to chat while waiting for the bus together and on the ride. If your campaign is about traffic violence, urge the decision-maker to meet with you at the dangerous spot and point out every speeder. For bike issues, it can be a bit tricky to get a government official to come on a bike ride with you, but the closer you can get them to having the same physical experience of a person on a bike, the better. Guiding the decision-maker through their own experience with your issue works wonders for helping your message sink in.

For example, in Roanoke, Virginia, many of the bus stops predate the Americans with Disabilities Act (ADA) and often don't have sidewalks or a landing pad where a bus can put down its ramp.[12] Because of that inaccessible design, wheelchair users often can't access bus stops' boarding zones. Disability justice advocate Steve Grammer, who gets around via a power wheelchair and often speaks through an interpreter, invited his city's vice mayor to join him for a bus ride with fellow members of the Bus Riders of Roanoke Advocacy Group. In our interview, he said: "The vice mayor rode the bus with me and noticed that the main bus stops are not accessible. . . . I felt like it brought awareness to the city, so they know what it's like for the disability community to ride the bus." Having the real-world experience of trying to board an inaccessible bus sticks with a person far more than reports and statistics. Grammer's actions planted the seed for change, and his continued advocacy alongside the Bus Riders of Roanoke Advocacy Group will one day make the Roanoke bus system truly accessible to all.[13]

Bringing the inside out can create real moments of human connection between decision-makers and advocates that wouldn't happen in a meeting on Zoom or in an office. For example, multiple elected officials biked to an event as part of a bike celebration in my community. The event was a great way to make some personal connections with the elected officials, and it helped them open up about their biking-related experiences. At that event, every single elected official spoke freely about how they want to see more protected bike lanes. One even opened up about his own experience hitting a cyclist when driving—although the cyclist was not seriously harmed, the official pointed out how it wouldn't have happened with a protected bike lane. While I wouldn't say the admission slipped out of him, I don't think he would have been as open if he hadn't just biked for a bit around town. When we bring politicians outside and out of their comfort zones, we can open their eyes to see the world more like we do.

In addition to bringing inside people out, we can bring inside information out. In the Burlingame example, if an agency staffer had told an outside supporter that the city hadn't yet done any outreach to promote the car-free block party, it would have set off alarm bells. With enough lead time to get the community excited, outside organizers could have made the event a success. All it would have taken is getting a pivotal piece of information from the inside to the outside.

It is on both the insiders and the outsiders to open lines of communication with one another. If you are an outsider, you can facilitate this by, in the words of Bill Nesper of the League of American Bicyclists, "hav[ing] an actual relationship with the people who are tasked with the planning, design, and implementation of the projects you are advocating for."[14] If you are the government staffer or consultant working on the project, you can build relationships with your potential allies on the outside. Agency staffers are generally free to share publicly available information that can help demystify the inside process to outsiders. For example, an insider can help outside partners by laying out all the steps in the official decision-making process and identifying who is officially involved with each one.

Josh, the urban planning consultant and host of the urban planning YouTube channel Radical Planning, explained in our interview that agency staffers can also help outside advocates with a nudge. It can be "as simple as suggesting, 'Why don't you look into this?' to an advocate group or to a journalist and let them take it from there." If you're concerned about engaging in an activity that may or may not be approved by your employer, Josh assured that "leaks are extremely common to the point that I haven't really seen a planning department attempt to rein [them] in."[15] But when talking about government information that is not yet public, it's always a good idea to use some common sense.

Independent Together

A third way inside/outside games can collaborate is by being "independent together." In these situations, they each do their own thing, but in a coordinated way so that it works better than if they had been operating truly independently. In the previous chapter, I mentioned a campaign during which outside activists blocked a freeway to highlight the need for transit funding while inside advocates directly lobbied the governor's office on the topic. Moments like this work when the inside and outside players are making a demand that is effectively the same, using similar messaging, and the timing syncs up. Ideally, the outsiders cause a ruckus that gets the decision-maker's attention, and the insiders are able to sit down with the decision-maker's office to talk things through.

Syncing Up the Inside/Outside Game

Syncing up the insiders and outsiders can be tricky because inside and outside players can be fundamentally different. Those distinctions can be an obvious source of tension. As Bill Nesper says, outsiders can view insiders as "fuddy-duddies," and in return, insiders can view outsiders as rabble-rousers.[16] It's a classic "odd couple" pairing, and the key is for each to accept the other as they are. From there, they can build a productive working relationship. Much like being an effective coalition partner, being effective inside/outside partners involves keeping each other informed about your constraints and respecting your partners' expertise when it comes to making change in their lane. If you are an outsider, trust that the insiders know how to win on the inside and vice versa.

The inside and outside partners are experts in their respective fields,

Figure 6.1. Inside/outside strategy in action. *Credit:* Fern K. Hahn

but they are rarely experts in both. "Everyone's an expert in their own experience" is one of the ground rule reminders I heard from Nailah Pope-Harden, former executive director of ClimatePlan, a network of climate-focused organizations working in California. I participated in the coalition meetings she led where she frequently navigated inside/outside game dynamics. She always started the coalition meetings with some reminders to facilitate a collaborative mindset and minimize potential misunderstandings. Remembering that everyone is an expert in their thing, including you, sets the stage for richer collaboration. You may encounter an obstacle that is beyond you, but another partner's expertise can help you overcome it. Ask and see what your partners think they can do. Similarly, tell them what you could do.

Sometimes inside/outside coordination requires some respectful nudging of your partners to remind them that you have different abilities than they do. If a partner says that a decision-maker won't support your issue, they may actually mean, "I can't get the decision-maker to care using the resources I have at my disposal, and I have not considered the ways you could change the situation." Help them see the situation through the eyes of the *coalition* and not just their own group.

Common Stumbling Blocks

Inside/outside campaigns are powerful, but there are a lot of moving parts. Insiders and outsiders can both drop the ball. Let's take a brief look at why that might happen and how to prevent it.

How the Inside Game Can Drop the Ball

Some mistakes insiders can make include fumbling the negotiations, focusing more on their access rather than their impact, or providing faulty intelligence to coalition partners. One of the most important roles of inside partners is to be at the negotiating table with the decision-makers and other stakeholders. This is more than just a regular lobby meeting; this is a high-pressure situation where the deal is struck between the campaign and the decision-maker. Inside coalition partners can mess up at the negotiation table by settling for something different or smaller than the coalition was prepared to settle for. Your coalition can lower the risk of an inside partner going rogue by having multiple inside partners at the negotiating table. That said, too many cooks in the kitchen can lead to a lack of cohesion among the insiders, allowing decision-makers to point to a divided constituency as an excuse to refuse to take action. But when inside partners communicate clearly about the status of negotiations, and when inside and outside partners function as a team, they can avoid these pitfalls.

Inside allies can also make the mistake of prioritizing their access to decision-makers over making change. Insiders' access to decision-makers is based on having a relationship with the decision-maker, and when a decision-maker is unhappy with what inside advocates' outside allies are doing, the decision-maker can revoke access. To keep their access, some insiders try to tamp down the outside's actions or, worse, try to protect the decision-maker from outside pressure. This can look like a bike advocacy group applauding a new but woefully inadequate bike lane, to the frustration of people who want safe bike lanes. If the inside actors are accepting crumbs now in order to win a bigger piece of the pie later, it may not be a bad strategy. But given the relatively few transformational wins in transportation advocacy, that strategy of delayed gratification does not seem to be working well. This dynamic can be avoided by remembering that the purpose of access is to use it to effect change. It's also solved by having a robust outside game that refuses to be silenced by the inside game.

Finally, inside-game actors can misstep by providing bad intelligence back to the coalition. This mainly happens when the inside game can't get a good read on the situation, doesn't actually have as much access as they think they do, or falls for a lie. The most common way bad intelligence hurts a campaign is when the inside game assures the outside game that everything is under control when it isn't. If insiders wrongly tell outsiders they can prematurely stop pressuring a decision-maker, the campaign may slow down at a time when it actually needs to ramp up. Campaigns can prevent this issue by improving the sophistication of the inside game and maintaining active outside organizing.

When the Outside Game Missteps

When either the inside or the outside game makes a mistake, it tends to come from misreading the situation. For the outside game, one way their misreading of the situation can hurt the campaign is when they do something that delegitimizes the campaign, making it look unserious in the eyes of the decision-maker. When the inside game has to spend time apologizing or distancing themselves from the outside game's actions, the campaign is squandering its energies.

While sometimes outside activists' actions can get in the way of the campaign's success, concerns about this are often overblown. Pretty much every time you shut down traffic for a political action—like hosting a big bike ride—someone will say you are hurting your cause. While it may hurt your cause in their eyes, it may help your cause in the eyes of others. Evaluate the merit of a potential action by considering if it will produce the outcomes the campaign needs at that moment. Chapter 7 describes how to do that in more detail. When you are taking on car dominance, there will nearly always be an opponent who tries to paint your outside game's actions as bothersome, counterproductive, or even fraudulent—no matter how you act. Drown out your haters by building a big and diverse coalition of allies.

The outside game can also make the inside game look weak in the eyes of the decision-maker by overpromising or failing to follow through on flexing their muscle. For example, the outside partners could promise to back up the inside partners with a big rally or other large action. But if they only muster a meager showing, that allows the decision-maker to discount the inside partners, and the campaign may lose its authority. This has a straightforward solution: Communicate accurately about what you can do and keep your partners informed.

One of the most important roles of the outside game is to continuously build pressure on the decision-maker, so another way the outside game falters is by failing to stay mobilized. Even if the campaign's focus shifts to the inside, don't go totally quiet on the outside. This is an especially common mistake for outside advocates who have gained a level of inside access and then feel that they no longer need to apply outside pressure on the decision-makers. Outside-game mobilization takes a while to build up momentum. Keep the outside game going, even at a diminished capacity, and ramp up from there when needed. It is much easier to do this than it is to let the fire go out and try to jump-start things later. If you want to win big, absolutely do not pack up your outside organizing and call it a day.

There are many ways to keep the flame of the outside game alive. As covered in chapter 2, one way is to wage multiple efforts at once. The simplest way to do this is to aim the outside game at an upcoming hurdle the inside game will face. On the Bay Bridge bus lane campaign I led, when the focus shifted to writing the bill and the internal negotiations, we kept the outside game building by focusing it on lining up support from other lawmakers in the region. By the time the inside game got the bill ready to be introduced, the outside game had already generated the pressure needed from the community to line up lots of support from other lawmakers. It helped that we had brought people up the ladder of engagement into campaign leadership roles to share the workload.

Simple Strategies, Simple Actions, Big Results

Once you get the hang of it, you may start to notice inside/outside team-ups in all sorts of contexts outside of activism, because at its core, the strategy is about collaborating across different positions to achieve a common goal.

In this chapter, we discussed how to win change through different roles and approaches, and how to coordinate across them to win even bigger. In prior chapters, you learned about the nature of transportation politics, thought about some fights you might want to wage, and considered how to adjust your advocacy to fit your context and make connections. You may have started thinking about forming up your core team and coming up with a list of potential coalition partners to reach out to. And now you know how to deploy an inside/outside strategy to pressure decision-makers even more effectively. You have the frameworks, theories, and strategies in place. It's time to get into the nuts and bolts of a campaign's actions. Let's talk tactics.

Action Points

1) Write out some potential decision-makers and influencers your campaign will seek to sway. For each one, consider how hard or easy you think it might be to get in front of them for a conversation.
2) Sign up for your local elected official's email list or follow them on social media so you can learn about upcoming public events they will attend. Go to one of those events and introduce yourself to the elected official in a friendly manner. If they did something you like, tell them. Your goal is just to make a connection with them on a shared value. This connection may be the seed of your inside access.
3) Consider your potential role in an inside/outside strategy. Which role do you think you would be more comfortable in? From that position, how could you support someone in the other role?
4) Check out a relevant transportation advocacy group that covers your area or state. Read their website, social media, and/or emails with an eye for how they are trying to bring people on the outside (in this case, you) into the process of winning change. When they put out action alerts on things you agree with, take action.

CHAPTER 7

Deploying Tactics to Win

We relied on actual relationships in our outreach. We encouraged our members to reach out personally to their own state senators and actively avoided form emails and fancy systems designed to support lobbying efforts.—Luke Hoffman, executive director of the Iowa Bicycle Coalition[1]

To achieve a campaign's goals and meet its needs, campaigners create strategies that are put into action through activities known as tactics. This chapter showcases a range of tactics transportation advocacy campaigns can implement, with real-world examples and tips on best practices. Pick and choose tactics based on what you need.

Since there are so many tactics at your disposal, let's start with how to evaluate a tactic to see if it fits your campaign's needs. You can ask yourself the questions in box 7.1 to evaluate a tactic.

The tactics in this chapter include those most commonly used in transportation campaigns. Each tactic produces multiple outcomes, so here the tactics are categorized based on the need they *primarily* serve. The first category is bringing people into the campaign. As earlier chapters covered, you cannot win alone and winning takes a lot of work, so your campaign needs to bring people in. The second category covers

Box 7.1: Questions to Evaluate a Tactic

- What immediate outcomes are likely from this tactic?
- Does the campaign need those outcomes at this time?
- What will it take to deploy the tactic?
- Are the likely outcomes worth the effort involved in producing them?
- Is the campaign capable of deploying that tactic? If not, what would the campaign need to do to position itself to be capable?
- What other tactics could produce the same desired outcomes?

tactics that apply pressure on the decision-maker, because you can't win if you don't push for it. When done right, the tactics you choose create a virtuous cycle of building power, which enables you to apply more pressure, which generates more attention, which draws in more people, which allows you to apply even more pressure.

Bringing People into the Campaign

The more people who get involved, the more powerful the campaign will be. Each person who gets involved in the effort brings energy, relationships, and other resources into the campaign.

Tactic to Bring People In: Making and Circulating a Petition

A petition is a public statement of your demand, often in the format of a message to the decision-maker that people can sign to show their support. Petitions are excellent tools for bringing people into the effort because when a person signs your petition and provides their contact information, they move up the first rung of the ladder of engagement.

For example, ProgressNow New Mexico and Together for Brothers circulated a petition in 2023 to demand that the Albuquerque city government make public transit free. Nearly 1,500 people—mainly Albuquerque residents (Burqueños)—signed the petition, which allowed the campaigners to demonstrate the strong level of community support for their demand. The campaigners won, and public transit is now free in Albuquerque.[2] The petition was in Spanish and English, and I've included the English-version text in boxes 7.2, 7.3, and 7.4 with my commentary in parentheses and *italics* to highlight the lessons you can apply to your own petition writing.

The online petition required signers to provide their first name, last name, email address, zip code, and city. There's space for people to opt into providing their cell phone number and additional comments. Gathering a person's contact information gives you the ability to add them to your database and contact them about other campaign activities, a crucial way to build your base of supporters. In transportation campaigns, collecting people's zip code and city helps demonstrate to the decision-maker that the signers are their constituents, the people they are elected to represent.

Online petitions are better than paper petitions for managing your database of signers. When setting up an online petition, pick a petitioning tool that allows you to download your signers' contact information so you can contact them later. Remember, people should be able to opt out of further contact if they want. Some tools for petition management that let you keep the signers' contact information include Action Network, NationBuilder, and Google Forms (which connects to Google Sheets). Once a person signs the petition, you can ask them to encourage other people to sign it in order to get the petition further out into the world, as depicted in figure 7.1.

Once you have a petition ready to share with the public, get people to sign it by putting it out to your community through online posts, in-person outreach, and digital outreach such as email and text and direct messages. You can distribute a print or digital petition standing on the sidewalk, on the bus, or at an intersection. As transportation advocates, we have a natural advantage in our in-person petitioning: We can

Box 7.2: Beginning of a Petition

Dear Albuquerque City Councilors,

I urge you to support funding the Zero Fares transit pilot program through June 2023.

(Your petition should be addressed to the decision-makers who can implement your demand. Note: This petition included a specific and time-limited demand, but they ended up winning more than what they initially demanded, expanding the pilot program indefinitely.)

Box 7.3: Middle of a Petition

Since implementing the Zero Fares in January 2022, Albuquerque has eliminated the biggest barrier for Burqueños to ride the bus—fares. Zero Fares spurs positive impacts for transit riders, businesses, and the city as well.

- Transit riders are predominantly people of color, live on low incomes, and/or do not have access to a personal vehicle. Zero Fares allows them to stretch their budgets with zero-cost transportation to school, work, and recreation.
- Transit riders now have increased access to food and shopping, benefitting the city economy.
- The City of Albuquerque's Zero Fares program has eliminated the need and cost of fare-collecting resources and the burden that fare collection previously placed on bus drivers.
- Community organizations that historically purchased and gave away bus passes, can now reallocate those funds ($1.6M over the past three years) to better support their clients.
- In alignment with the City's Climate Action, Zero Fares helps reduce the 47% of carbon emissions attributed to surface travel, mitigating the harmful effects of climate change.

(Contextualize the problem and reaffirm the solution you are demanding. Connect it to the decision-makers' values and clearly state who benefits from solving the problem. Highlight a diverse range of benefits.)

Box 7.4: Ending of a Petition

The pilot project for Zero Fares needs to be multi-year as it is in all other U.S. cities that have launched Zero Fares. Multi-year funding for Zero Fares ensures time for

- Community outreach/communications
- Collecting rider stories and feedback, and
- Full quantitative and qualitative analysis of how Zero Fares fits into the overall plan for a city's public transportation infrastructure.

The more time for the Zero Fares, the better for understanding the full impact—economically, socially, and environmentally.

I believe that Albuquerque can and should be a leader in working towards a resilient and equitable transit system. I am asking City Council members to support the continuation of the Zero Fares pilot project for all Albuquerque transit riders through June 2023.[a]

(*Elaborate on why the solution you propose is the right one and back up your reasoning. End with a summary of the specific demand and why it matters.*)

a. "Sign the Petition: Support Zero Fares Transit ABQ into 2023," ProgressNow New Mexico, 2023, https://progressnownm.actionkit.com/sign/zero-fares-for-all-abq_2023.

often literally point out the problem our petition seeks to solve, which makes it easier to inspire people to sign on. Another common in-person petitioning tactic is tabling, where you set up a table in a populated area like a farmer's market and use it as a base for engaging people. The table is for setting up a little information stand; you should stand by it and talk to people. You can sit next to the table if you want, but sitting behind the table separates you from the people you are trying to connect with.

Chapter 3 discussed how contexts affect advocacy, and that is particularly true when it comes to advocates' experiences while petitioning or otherwise engaging with strangers in public. In a blog post about what organizers can do to make their campaigns safer for all, organizer and

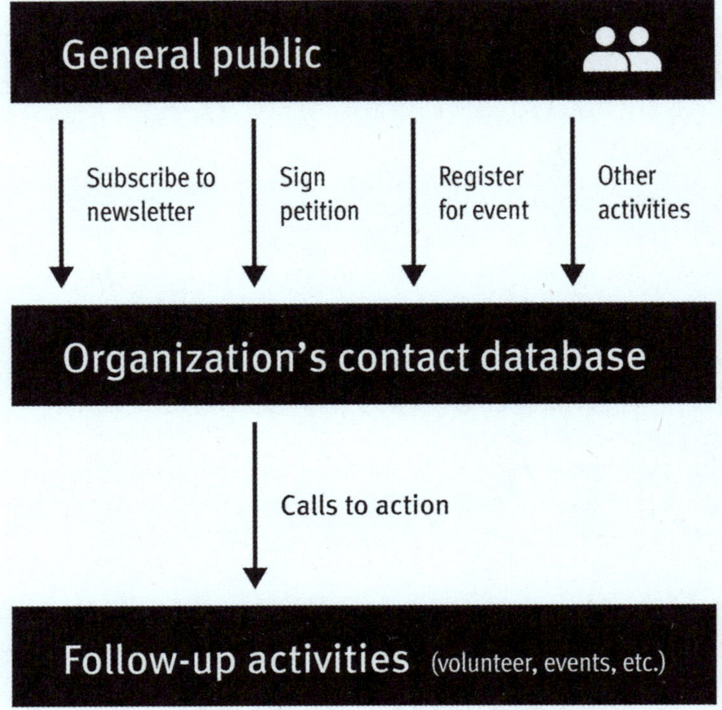

Figure 7.1. A workflow for helping the people who join the campaign get more people involved. *Credit:* Fern K. Hahn

campaign consultant Izzy Goodman wrote about the complexities that women and people of color face while walking and knocking on doors to talk with neighbors about political issues—a tactic known as canvassing. Her tips and lessons about door-to-door canvassing generally apply to other forms of outreach in the community, like tabling or passing out flyers. Here are some of her recommendations that are most relevant for transportation advocates:

- "**Make it clear who you are to the community**" with shirts, signs, buttons, or some other indicator so when someone sees you they can understand who you are and what you are doing.

- "**Recruit people to canvass their own neighborhoods.** This means canvassers are more likely to know their neighbors, know who to avoid, and you have the added benefit of many of these contacts being relational."
- "**Assign people (or let people pick) canvassing buddies.**"
- "**Be explicit about the role**" and what people are expected to do. When asking people to help out, getting their "enthusiastic consent is important."[3]

Tactic to Bring People In: Flyering

A flyer can be the first point of connection a person has with your campaign. You can use flyers to educate people, invite them to an event, or encourage them to take a simple action like signing a petition. Flyers need to include the essential information you want to get across while being easy to understand. When making a flyer, include concise, nontechnical language; a compelling and relevant image; and your organization's name. Figure 7.2 shows an example of an effective flyer from a 2024 BikePGH (Pittsburgh) effort for traffic safety improvements.

BikePGH's advocacy manager Seth Bush broke down the elements that made this flyer effective: "It has an eye-catching graphic that makes it immediately obvious what the problem is: The bike lane ends. It has a values statement that folks can easily get behind. There's a catchy campaign name with good design and both a link and QR code where folks can sign a petition." Volunteers handed out the small flyer during times of high pedestrian traffic in the surrounding area. He says, "We got a lot of petition signatures, which we mobilized for a packed public meeting . . . that led to enough momentum to start up a new bike/ped [bike and pedestrian] committee in the area."[4] When you're sharing a flyer to inform people about a campaign or an event, make sure others can see it by putting it out in relevant high-traffic places, whether they are physical or digital. Directly giving or sending it to someone is even more effective.

Figure 7.2. A flyer from Bike PGH's campaign for street safety improvements in the Strip District. *Credit:* BikePGH

Tactic to Bring People In: Making and Circulating a Coalition Sign-On Letter

Chapter 5 briefly discussed coalition sign-on letters as a tool for assembling a coalition. A coalition sign-on letter is similar to a petition, but instead of individual people signing on to the letter, organizations or groups (or people representing those groups) sign on to it. Your coalition letter can be nearly identical to your petition, but the letter may have a section explaining who the signers are, such as "We, the undersigned groups," or "As houses of worship, businesses, environmental organizations, and transportation advocates, we urge . . ." or whichever types of groups you're seeking to sign the letter.

Circulate the sign-on letter by sending it to potential coalition partners and asking if they would sign on. When they say yes, add their logo and organization name to the document, and consider including the name and title of the person who signed on behalf of the organization. Later on, we'll discuss delivering these letters.

Tactic to Bring People In: Campaigning Online

Politics is about people, so it's important to campaign where the people are. Even if you are just trying to win a small change, like a new crosswalk, establishing an online presence can be a low-effort investment that pays dividends.

One way to reach people online is to develop a presence on social media. Before you jump in, consider who your audience is, which platforms they use, and what you are trying to get from your social media efforts. Your campaign or group's social media presence can help create a steady drumbeat of activity to grow your audience and keep them educated, engaged, and primed for more action.

For example, while working to get light-rail built in Atlanta, Georgia, the group Atlanta Beltline Rail Now produced a series of short Instagram videos that acted as micro-commercials showcasing a diverse range of business owners, disability justice advocates, local politicians, and other supporters of the rail line. While the videos are polished enough to be easy to watch, they are still very clearly the work of passionate grassroots activists. The group's steady trickle of videos, each with anywhere from dozens to hundreds of likes or comments, puts its campaign in front of supporters, introduces the campaign to new people, and keeps people tuned in for alerts about events like rallies to jolt the mayor into action.

If your campaign or group will last more than a few weeks, it may be a worthwhile investment to set up a website as well. Start with a basic page and add more as you need. Your website should explain the campaign and why it matters, and provide people with an opportunity to get involved. Link to your petition and your coalition sign-on letter when they are public. Since we live in an era of computer-generated spam, it's important to show that your group is, in fact, real. Post positive write-ups about your efforts in the media, pictures of the group in action (like tabling), and a section on the website about who you and your group are. Providing that information about your group helps show that you aren't fake or just a one-person operation. Your website can also be a resource for educating your community about the change you are advocating for. Consider linking to YouTube explainers, National Association of City Transportation Officials (NACTO) diagrams, books, or other content about the type of change you seek while adding context about your specific campaign to help teach people about your vision.

Applying Pressure on the Decision-Maker

Most transportation campaigns require decision-makers to buck the status quo, which is hard. "If you want someone to prioritize your work and your needs, then make it the easiest option for them out of all of their options," says José Antonio Zayas Cabán, executive director of the Minneapolis, Minnesota–based transportation advocacy group Our Streets.[5] As covered in chapter 6, you can help a decision-maker on the inside so it is easier for them to prioritize your demand. Another way to help them prioritize your demand is by pressuring them on the outside. Pressuring a politician is the act of making it hard to say no to you. If they initially think saying yes to you is a bad move for their political career, make sure they know saying no to you is far worse.

Tactic to Apply Pressure: Publicly Making the Official Ask

If you want to win a change, you need to ask for it. Put the decision-maker in the spotlight so they have to make a public choice: side with your campaign or actively choose to maintain the status quo. While you can make your official ask via a public comment during the official process, in a private meeting with the decision-maker or their staff, or over a phone call or email, your campaign can also make the ask in a way that puts the decision-maker in the spotlight. In fact, you are already building up to that big moment. Your petition and coalition letter are addressed to the decision-maker: Deliver them! When you do, bring a crowd and media with you, and it'll be very hard for the decision-maker to say no. When planning to deliver your petition or coalition letter to the decision-maker, the main elements to consider are the story, timing, and logistics.

Tell a Story

Your campaign is a story; it is a series of connected actions that form a narrative. The story might center on a problem you and your allies have gathered together to solve. Your story might be about a vision for a better future you are trying to bring about. The start of your campaign is the beginning of its story. The building up of the campaign is the story's middle. But the ending is still to be determined. You need to make your demand of the decision-maker to find out what the ending is.

The delivery of your petition or coalition letter is likely the climax of the story. It is the moment where you have marshaled a bunch of power and are reaching out to the decision-maker without knowing how they will respond, so make your delivery eye-catching and newsworthy by crafting a clear story around it. Collaborate with your team to determine which story will be the most impactful to tell through the action. At this early stage in your transportation campaign, your decision-maker is likely not the "villain" of the story, but rather the potential hero who has yet to step up. That may change depending on how they react to this event, but you want to engage them in good faith at first rather than alienate them.

Here are some ways to heighten the drama of delivering your demands:

- Give reporters and the general public a hook so they understand why your demand is important and why they should care.
- Deliver a notable number of signatures backing the demand.
- Bring a big, diverse crowd with you, especially leaders from groups in your coalition.
- Deliver your demand in a visually striking way with props and an interesting setting. For example, you can deliver a huge stack of petition signatures to the decision-maker in their office with a crowd of people holding signs.
- Think of the moment through the lens of a camera. Consider matters such as who is in the shot, what they are doing, and what's behind them. Make sure there are a lot of people in the shot so people who see it on the news realize there is a supportive crowd there. Aim to make it so that a single picture from the event can convey the key message from the day to anyone who sees it. Recruit someone to take photos and let them know what images you would like them to capture, also known as your "shot list."
- Film it and invite the media along for the show. (We'll cover media relations more below.)
- Do it at the right moment.

Timing

Time your delivery so that it's as newsworthy as possible. If there is a pivotal public committee hearing on your topic, deliver your demands in the run-up to it. If there aren't any scheduled meetings about your topic, you get to decide when you want to make a splash. Relevant events—like the children's group ride Kidical Mass or Transit Month—are also opportunities to build on as people are primed to think about your topic.

Be careful when considering doing an event in response to the death of a local bicyclist or pedestrian. People and communities who have lost loved ones to traffic violence have a range of responses and are in a vulnerable position: Do not put them or their pain into the spotlight without their consent. Having been involved with several vigils and commemorative actions in response to traffic violence deaths, I believe they are some of the most complicated, high-stakes, and emotionally fraught actions an activist can engage in. Proceed with extreme caution.

For most issues, however, it is always a good time to demand improvements. There are also times when decision-makers are particularly open to hearing what we have to say. Earlier chapters discussed how your campaign will operate within the context of the decision-making process. For example, governors tend to draft the state budget at certain times of year, and legislators are up against various deadlines to get bills introduced and passed within the legislative calendar. Use that to your advantage.

Logistics

When preparing for events such as petition deliveries, make a run-of-show document that walks through the event or action step-by-step and minute-by-minute. This exercise will help you firm up your plan. It will also bring up questions that need to be resolved in the planning stage, like "What do we do if we can't get into the decision-maker's office for the delivery?" Work with your team of co-leaders and close coalition partners to sort out the logistics of your action so that it goes smoothly. Part of ensuring that the action goes smoothly is having backup plans and a clear understanding of who on your team is responsible for what.

Tactic to Apply Pressure: Building Relationships with Relevant Reporters

Media coverage of your issue turns up the heat on decision-makers who care about their public image. Even if you're not directly pressuring your decision-maker in the media, Beth Osborne explains, "if your topic keeps coming up in the news, they're going to pay attention to it."[6] Osborne said in our interview, "Let's say you want to build a complete street [a street that prioritizes people over cars] and the elected official said, 'No, let's keep the cars moving.' Then you make sure the press covers every single crash. . . . Make it so the reporter asks that elected person why speed is so important that it's worth killing so many people."[7]

By building relationships with reporters, you can shape the overall conversation around your issue and influence what your decision-maker thinks about it. Transportation issues aren't mainstream, so politicians, reporters, and the general public don't usually spend a lot of time thinking about them. Because our campaigns for non-car-centric transportation changes are rare, they often incite curiosity. The curiosity may be tinged with some condescension or skepticism, but it's still curiosity, which means eyeballs for media outlets.

You can use that curiosity and general lack of understanding by filling in that information gap and trying to define the issues on your terms. For example, if you want your transit agency to implement all-door bus boarding, you can introduce it as the amazing, high-tech, time-saving innovation that it is. By giving a reporter a framework to think about the issue, you can profoundly shape their eventual coverage of it. An example of a public relations fight on a transportation issue is the push to have reporters cover car crashes as "crashes" or "traffic violence" rather than "accidents." When you win the media framing of the issue, your campaign gains significant cultural power, especially relative to potential opponents.

A key thing to keep in mind when contacting reporters is that they are looking for things to cover. Your outreach isn't burdening them; you're making their jobs easier. Activists give reporters stories and information, and reporters put activists in the spotlight, so it can be a symbiotic relationship. To become a useful and trusted source for reporters, provide them with relevant potential news stories, help them learn about transportation issues, and connect them with other useful sources. Even if you are just being interviewed "on background," where you won't be quoted but you are educating a reporter about your issue, you have the opportunity to shape the coverage of the topic in your favor. Reporters are always up against a deadline, so the more they feel like they can turn to you to get their needs met quickly, the more they will.

A good first step when connecting with reporters is to look up who's already writing about transportation issues in your area or writing about your decision-maker. Read some pieces they have written so you can reference those when first reaching out to them. If your area does not have a transportation reporter, remember that your transportation issue has a business connection, a local politics connection, and a "human interest" or local news connection, all of which are topics covered by reporters. In addition to reaching out via email, you can find reporters on social media and share their articles, comment on their posts, and tag them when posting about your campaign online. Through your research and experience, you may get a sense that a reporter or outlet is "friendly"—and will try to make your campaign look good—or "hostile"—and will try to make you look bad. Plan accordingly.

Keep in mind, anything you say to a reporter is fair game for them to put in the news, so if you want to have a conversation with them where they agree to not put what you say in the news, you can ask them for the conversation to be "off the record." *It is only off the record if the reporter agrees.* A hostile reporter might not respect that agreement, so be careful.

Tactic to Apply Pressure: Getting Reporters to Cover Your Events and Activities

You can also do mass outreach to reporters by sending out a press release, which is especially useful to invite them to cover an event or action of yours. A press release is essentially a short pre-written article submitted to a journalist to try to get their attention. Sometimes when a journalist gets a press release that piques their interest, they decide to write their own story on the topic, often using material from the press release. Since journalists get flooded with press releases, you need to cut through the noise by submitting newsworthy content in a digestible format. You can find sample press releases online to see what they look like and pick a format you like.

Once you have sent the press release to relevant reporters, follow up to confirm they received it. The public relations world is increasingly filled with spam, so make sure to add a human touch in order to stick out. Early on the morning of your big event, send out a reminder—especially to local TV news stations, which often have meetings very early in the morning to pick which of the day's stories to cover.

Take into account which type of media outlet you're talking with: If it's TV, they'll be interested in the visuals and the speakers at your event. Print or online newspapers may include some photos in their coverage, but if they don't send a photographer to your event, don't worry—you can send them photos afterward along with a brief recap. Radio reporters may come to capture the speeches and sounds, or you can ask to schedule an interview with them ahead of time to build anticipation for your event. You can also send them videos of the event they can pull audio from to include in their broadcasts.

Much like in your outreach to coalition partners, remember that reporters are incredibly busy. They may not respond at all, or their plans might change at the last minute. This may be frustrating to you, but do not burn bridges. While your short-term goal might be to get coverage of a particular action, remember that your campaign and organizing will likely last a while. When working with reporters, especially local reporters, remember to cultivate a mutually beneficial relationship for the long term.

Your campaign has to compete for attention with everything else the reporter could cover. Fortunately, as activists, we have a leg up over other people who want to be in the news: We get to create news. Organizing an interesting demonstration is an excellent way to get the media's attention, and it is even more effective if you tell reporters what your plans are ahead of time so they know when and where they should be to capture the story. Escalating actions are also excellent tactics for ratcheting up the pressure on a decision-maker.

Tactic to Apply Pressure: Escalating

There may come a point in your campaign where your team has built power, applied it, and made your demands public, but things haven't changed. As covered in the previous chapters, we need decision-makers to say more than "yes"; we need them to follow through with action. If they haven't said yes or they haven't yet followed through, you can escalate your campaign to make it a higher priority for decision-makers.

The general public may be confused as to why you are escalating, so make sure your escalation is clearly justifiable. For example, in 2024, New York Governor Kathy Hochul suddenly paused the proposed congestion charge for Manhattan below 60th Street before it went into effect, after it had been in the works for years. The charge was supposed to play a pivotal role in funding much-needed transit improvements in the city while reducing traffic violence and congestion. Numerous detailed studies and articles had thoroughly vetted the proposed charge, and the issue was top of mind for many in the area. So, the community was shocked by Governor Hochul's last-minute pause of the charge. It was a drastic action on her part, which merited a drastic escalation in response. Activists immediately rose to the occasion with a flurry of protests, articles, and street art, and they won![8] Like the New Yorkers advocating for a congestion charge, you may find that you need to escalate your campaign. We can do that in a few ways: intensifying what we say, how we say it, and the consequences we deal out to the decision-maker for ignoring us. We can also do all three at once.

Escalation Tactic: Intensifying What You Say

When intensifying your campaign message in order to escalate the pressure on the decision-maker, consider your audience's current level of understanding of the issue. Meet your audience where they are and then bring them to a more intense feeling about the situation through your updated messaging. For example, when starting a campaign for street safety, your campaign may launch with an initial message to potential supporters such as "Tell the mayor to build speed bumps." This message is fairly neutral and easy to understand for a person hearing it for the first time. Eventually, during the campaign, it may become clear to you that the mayor has gotten the message and yet continues to ignore the demand. You may want to respond by intensifying your message to the community about the mayor's negligence, but keep in mind that your supporters might not know that the mayor is ignoring the demand. So, when escalating, explain to your supporters why escalation is necessary and provide evidence. For example, after the campaign has delivered the initial ask and gotten no response, then it is easy to justify an escalated message like "Tell the mayor: Stop ignoring our community's demand for safer streets!"

Help people adjust to the escalated message by helping them understand how your message suits the situation. The greater the escalation, the more justification you need to provide so people don't think you're freaking out for no reason. For example, you might feel that the mayor has blood on their hands for not implementing the traffic safety solutions that you have been demanding. However, if that's not the public's understanding of the situation, such an intense message may lose a lot of people. First you have to help your community move beyond viewing traffic violence as a random or inevitable tragedy so they can see that it is a solvable problem. From there, you can highlight who has the power to solve it and what they are (or aren't) doing about it. Then it is easier for people to understand that by ignoring your demands, the decision-maker is failing to protect your community. Once people see that the solutions you are pushing would save lives, and that the mayor is refusing to use their powers to enact those solutions, people *might* be open to the message that the mayor has blood on their hands.

When planning your escalated message, make sure to leave the decision-maker with an "exit pathway" they can use to declare a win or change course and side with you. Otherwise, you may box them in. If they have no incentive to agree with you, they might double down on disagreeing with you. For example, if you are demanding ten speed bumps on a road, the decision-maker may refuse at first. If you escalate by saying that the decision-maker is evil, they are unlikely to want to deal with you at all, and you lose out on the chance of winning even one speed bump. As transportation advocates, we rarely have the power needed to completely end a politician's career, so if we say that they can never make us happy, they may ignore us. Know what you would settle for and be okay with thanking the decision-maker for taking some action toward your goal. If separate groups are doing your campaign's inside and outside work, collaborate to figure out an acceptable exit pathway to build into your campaign for the decision-maker. Without that collaboration, it's possible that the inside/outside pressures will work at cross purposes on this matter.

While tactful escalation can ensure that your message isn't overly harsh, when you escalate by getting louder, a decision-maker can still tune you out if you are just doing the same stuff with the same people. In that case, escalate by changing up your playbook. Make your campaign unignorable.

Escalation Tactic: Disruption and Changing How You Get Your Message Across

Disrupting the current situation by changing how you get your message across helps grab people's attention. Confrontational actions like die-ins and street blockades are disruptions, which may get noticed by the public, the media, and your decision-maker. However, a disruptive action doesn't have to be big and loud; it can be as simple and powerful as a poem.

I witnessed the Antioch, California–based poet Moe Ministry deploy a poem to devastating effect. At a 2024 transit board hearing on cutting Amtrak service to her city, she joined over two dozen advocates (including myself) who wanted to keep the station open. Mayors of nearby towns, congressional staff, and other legislators also spoke out. But what seemed to get the transit board's attention the most was Moe Ministry's poem. Her beautiful piece cut to the emotional truth of the matter, and her powerful performance was a distinct stylistic departure from the other commenters. After her public comment/performance, a board member admitted that he recorded it so he could listen to it again. Her deviation from the norm ensured that her message got through.

Another attention-getting tactic is street theater, which can transform your community into your stage. Street theater is a natural fit for transportation campaigns because streets are part of our transportation system. This book's introduction mentioned an example of street theater deployed to stop California transit service cuts that would have set off a "death spiral," triggering a loss of riders and revenue that would in turn cause more service cuts. To get the funding needed to stop this death spiral, advocates created a statewide coalition, generated tens of thousands of petition signatures and calls into elected officials' offices, and directly lobbied officials in the capitol. But as the budget deadline loomed and the money was not forthcoming, it became clear that we needed to drastically escalate our actions. The coalition decided to organize a "transit funeral" with flower-draped caskets that had six-foot-long cardboard models of local buses and trains on top. San Francisco transit advocate Lian Chang says, "We figured this would make for good visuals for the media, and we were right!"[9] The funerary procession marched to the state office building in Oakland, where elected officials and community leaders spoke about how tragic the loss of transit would be. Then the processional rode the train to San Francisco, where more people joined in. After generating lots of news, including coverage in foreign press, the event significantly swayed the conversation in favor of transit.

But time was still running out. Though the private conversations in the capitol were reportedly turning in our direction, there was still no deal to save transit. So, the campaign escalated yet again—and outside leaders decided that we needed to make the message clear that this wasn't just a problem for transit riders. It would be a big problem for drivers if Governor Gavin Newsom killed transit because it would force more people onto the roads and cause traffic jams. Passionate people took it upon themselves to organize another protest where they blocked freeway traffic for several minutes as a protester in a Governor Newsom costume beat the heck out of a big cardboard train with a baseball bat. While drivers were stuck, the protester hammed it up for the social media livestream and the helicopter news footage. To make sure everyone got the right message, additional protesters held a big banner behind

"Governor Newsom" that said, "Gavin Newsom is killing transit." That way, if someone was wondering why the freeway was jammed, they had the answer right in front of them.

In the end, we got the $2 billion in proposed cuts revoked and helped win over $1 billion in additional transit funding for our state.

Remember: When crafting a disruptive action, make sure it generates sympathy for your cause as well as attention. Make it clear that the problem you are trying to bring attention to is bigger than the problem your disruption is causing. Some tactics are disruptive because they inconvenience the general public for a few minutes, like this freeway example. Some tactics are disruptive because they inconvenience the decision-makers themselves.

Escalation Tactic: Creating Electoral Consequences

You may want to escalate by ensuring that the decision-makers face direct electoral consequences for their actions. Show decision-makers that you will reward them if they do what you want them to do and that they'll have a hard time politically if they refuse you. If you do not create that clear behavioral feedback loop, you cannot expect elected decision-makers to react the way you want them to. Elected officials want to get reelected, and you have various tools at your disposal to leverage that fact.

Electoral Tactic: Candidate Questionnaires

A candidate questionnaire is a short series of questions about values and policies sent out to candidates for office. When candidates fill out the questionnaire and send it back to the group or coalition behind it, advocates can educate voters about the candidates' stances. A group can also use candidates' answers to inform its endorsement process. Creating a candidate questionnaire is particularly helpful for transportation advocates because candidates rarely have to go on the record about transportation issues. Most voters don't know what candidates think about buses, but if voters did, it might change how they vote. Additionally, questionnaires help show candidates that they should be thinking about transportation issues. I have co-led transportation questionnaire projects, and judging from the answers we receive, the questionnaire is clearly the first time some candidates have even considered transportation policy.

Managing a questionnaire project is straightforward:

1) Assemble a coalition to support and be involved in the questionnaire project. You can list coalition members when reaching out to candidates and when publicly putting out the results.
2) Collaborate with the coalition to write the questions for the candidates.
3) Make a spreadsheet of the electoral contest(s) you are targeting and collect the contact information of the candidates competing in each one.
4) Send the questionnaire to the candidates. Invite them to fill it out, give them a deadline, and explain what your coalition will do with the responses provided.
5) Follow up with candidates who haven't responded. Remind them of the deadline.
6) Once the deadline comes, compile and publish the candidates' responses. Send the compilation to your network and encourage the coalition partners to do the same. Put out a press release to encourage local media outlets to cover the project. Election-related news is often of interest to reporters.

Electoral Tactic: Donate Money

Candidates need donations so they can run their campaigns to connect with voters and win elections. Billionaires keep spending more on elections, and they are rarely funding candidates who support biking, transit, and street safety. It is hard for candidates who share your values to win when they are seriously outspent. When community advocates get electorally engaged, they can counteract that distortion of our democracy. If you like what a politician is doing on transportation issues, you can help get their campaign money so they can win the next election.

It's a straightforward symbiotic relationship, although there are a few important things to note to avoid trouble and maximize the return on your electoral investment. Warning: Direct payment for political favors is illegal. It's fine to host a fundraiser for a politician who has done good things on transit and it's fine to tell a politician that you like specific transit-related things they did, but it is illegal to directly promise to give a politician money in exchange for them doing a specific thing. For more information on campaign finance laws for individuals and nonprofit organizations, consult a lawyer.

With that in mind, without violating the law, make sure the politician knows who the money is coming from and why. For example, when you as a transportation activist organize a fundraiser for a candidate, they generally will get the hint that you like their transportation work. The donations don't have to come from your pocket: As transportation advocates, when we arrange for others to donate at a fundraiser we host, that sends the message to politicians that being good on transportation can get them campaign donations. Also, make sure your donations are proportional to the level of office the candidate is running for and to the level of effort you would like to see them put into your transportation issues. It takes a lot less money to get a local candidate's attention than it does to get on a senator's radar.

Electoral Tactic: Volunteer

Monetary donations only matter because they help move votes. Cut out the middleman by donating your time to help connect with voters as a way of rewarding candidates for their transportation stances. As Michael Wojcik with the Bicycle Alliance of Minnesota said about his time campaigning for city council, "I didn't have much money, but what I could do was knock on doors." Beyond knocking on doors for a candidate, actions like making an endorsement, hosting events with the candidate, or organizing a phone bank can also help you connect the candidate with voters. As is the case with donations, the important thing is that you make sure the politician knows why you are getting people to volunteer for their election. Keep in mind that if your group is an officially registered 501(c)(3) tax-exempt nonprofit organization, there are strict laws on what your group can do to help specific candidates. Consult a lawyer for details.

Electoral Tactic: Elevate Other Politicians

If a politician thwarts your dreams, consider returning the favor. When you actively back someone running against your decision-maker, you increase the pressure on the decision-maker. It is a risky move politically because if the candidate you are backing loses, you have dug yourself into a deep hole with the incumbent who remains the decision-maker. But if the incumbent is already saying no any time you ask for anything, you don't have much to lose by supporting someone else.

For example, bus rapid transit (BRT) advocates in Indianapolis threw their weight behind their state senator's opponent. They burned the bridge with the state senator in response to his unrepentant anti-BRT efforts and his deeply disrespectful actions toward advocates and constituents. Although the opponent lost, it was a fight worth losing, as explained by BRT advocate and Indianapolis city councilmember Jesse Brown prior to the election: "Even if we don't defeat him, we forced him to actually run a reelection campaign. . . . Even if you're winning by ten points, running for office is not a fun time. . . . That's going to influence [the state senator's] behavior in the future."[10]

A gentler approach is elevating other politicians who are not direct competitors of your decision-maker. When you shine a spotlight on a nearby politician who is good on transportation issues, you indirectly cast a bit of shade on others who haven't merited that same praise. This positive approach also keeps the door open to future collaboration with your decision-maker, and if they see how others have benefited from being on your good side, they might be more willing to work with you.

Adopt Tactics from Other Sources

For more ideas on tactics, consult the robust body of literature dedicated to grassroots movements. A personal favorite of mine is a book called *Beautiful Trouble: A Toolbox for Revolution* assembled by Andrew Boyd. The book distills campaign best practices, tactics, strategies, and theories from social movements around the world, presented in an encyclopedia format. Most of the campaigns covered aren't transportation centric, but the book includes some transportation-related campaigns, such as Brazil's 2013 Free Fare uprisings and Colombia's 1995 crackdown on traffic violence and police corruption, which temporarily replaced traffic cops with mimes.

As campaigns can be raucous environments, having effective tactics for meeting your campaign's internal needs will help your team do more and have an easier time doing it. There are some great books on managing volunteers and organizations, such as *The Empowerment Manual: A Guide for Collaborative Groups* by Starhawk and *Management in a Changing World: How to Manage for Equity, Sustainability, and Results* by Jakada Imani, Monna Wong, and Bex Ahuja.

After Your Campaign

Throughout campaigns, activists use strategies and tactics to build power and pressure decision-makers. Eventually, the decision-maker will make a decision. What your campaign needs to do in the next phase will depend on that decision.

If you win, congratulations! Well done. To make sure your victory gets implemented, stay on top of the process to confirm that the responsible parties are actually following through. Be prepared to crank up the heat in the event that they miss deadlines or hit other snags. As discussed in chapter 2, your transportation victory isn't complete until it gets fully implemented. Even then, it isn't truly over until the backlash has subsided. Once your change gets implemented, help the public learn to appreciate it.

If you don't win your campaign, that is unfortunate. The silver lining is that you will have still made progress and ended up stronger than when you started. Michael Wojcik says, "When you introduce a bill, even if it goes down, you still had the conversation, got the media coverage, and gained supporters."[11] After LINK Houston's push against a freeway expansion, Ines Sigel said, "Even though we were unable to fully stop the project, we got a lot of wins. Communities got some concessions. We got elected officials at the local, state, and federal level to think more deeply about a public transit system that works for everyone. Decision-makers now know that expanding freeways isn't going to be easy. People are going to speak out and force changes."[12] Beyond that particular campaign, the organization continues to push for better transportation in their area.

At the end of your campaign, whether you've won or lost, solidify your progress by wrapping things up nicely so that you start your next effort in a stronger position than you started your first one. A postmortem meeting of leaders and organizers creates an opportunity to aggregate and process what you have learned. Talk about what went well and what could be improved next time. Arrange and catalogue the knowledge you and your team have amassed over the campaign. Go through the notes, databases, lists, and other resources you have built together and inventory that information so you can access it later if needed. Your group will likely want to call again on the same potential coalition partners and the list of supporters, so make sure your databases are well organized. You will also have accumulated all sorts of things, like craft supplies or protest signs, photos and videos, people's contact information, and less tangible items like stories and connections. All of that can be useful to your next effort if you organize it in a way so that it is readily accessible when you need it in the future. A centralized inventory document will save you a lot of headaches when it comes to remembering what is where, in both the physical and digital worlds. Give your future self that gift.

As part of wrapping up your campaign, compile the story of the campaign. Share and take credit for victories—even if the victories aren't about change from your decision-maker but are instead about the power you built with allies and supporters. Those victories may include the number of petition signers your team got, the actions you put on, and the coalition you built. This affirms that the work everyone put in mattered and that although the campaign is over, its power carries on. You can also take this time to let supporters know you're looking ahead toward other campaigns in the future, which you'll update them about. You may want to have a party or other community gathering to celebrate your shared accomplishments.

Although your campaign for a specific transportation change may be over, you still have an open invitation to fight for a better world. Your transportation advocacy adventure can last your whole life if you choose. There is more than enough work for all of us, and your unique contribution to the movement makes the world a better place. You are already well on your way, and you have everything you need to win.

Action Points

1) Look back at the action points from the previous chapters and come back here once you have launched your campaign and you are ready for the next steps.
2) Make a plan with your allies for a petition and coalition letter delivery targeting the decision-maker.

3) Build a database of relevant media outlets and reporters, then send them a media advisory or press release inviting them to attend the delivery action.
4) Collectively deliver your demands to the decision-maker. Make a big show out of it and share photos from the event.
5) If necessary, regroup and escalate. Repeat until the decision-maker publicly makes their decision.
6) Spread the news about what the decision-maker did, what the impacts will be, and how your coalition feels about it.
7) Reflect on what you've learned and clean up your notes so you are prepared for your next campaign.

Conclusion

Big transit projects always span multiple electoral terms, and then rail projects span several decades. . . . When you are building an advocacy push, it needs to span decades. We need that advocacy to see itself in administration, in governing, as the elected official, as the politician's aide, and as the outside people pushing at the same time.—Irene Fernando, Hennepin County Commissioner[1]

Transportation advocates want big things. Winning the changes we want takes time and consistent effort in multiple arenas with periods of higher or lower intensity; that goes far beyond any one campaign. Your campaign—for a speed bump, bike lane, bus route, or whatever you believe in—will evolve in all sorts of directions. Along with the allies and coalition partners who join your efforts, you will collectively shape your broader community, and on a personal level, you will grow and become more politically strategic, a better communicator, and wiser. Each fight helps you get better at picking your battles and charting a pathway to win your dreams. Across campaigns, you'll learn more about your community and the cultural, political, and historical contexts you inhabit.

The political strength you build through your campaign will carry on, even when it ends. You still have the supporters, volunteers, leaders, and coalition partners you've assembled, and you still have everything you learned about campaigning. Regardless of the outcome, you will be in a significantly stronger position than when you first started. You can keep building on that for as long as you want, and this book will still be here to help.

Though your campaign may be over, there is always important work to be done to make our communities better. Figuring out how to sustain your advocacy is crucial. When your campaign wraps up, take a moment to check in with yourself and consider if now is the right time for you to keep on campaigning.

How Are You Feeling?

Advocacy is exhilarating and exhausting. If you finish your campaign revved up and ready for another round, wonderful! Stay with that feeling. In the likely event that you are exhausted, take that seriously. You've become a more experienced leader, and people may ask you to help with other advocacy projects. Before you recommit yourself to that treadmill of advocacy, consider two questions: Are you actually able to campaign again right now? And do you actually want to do it? Your next steps depend on the answers to those questions.

Able but Unmotivated

You might be fully capable of taking on another effort, but you may not feel like it. It can be demotivating if progress feels impossible or too slow—so find your power and find joy. A key step to get you going again is doing "anything that isn't nothing," Emily and Amelia Nagoski write in the book *Burnout: The Secret to Unlocking the Stress Cycle.*[2]

For transportation activists, it can be especially revitalizing to do something joyful that is connected to non-car transportation. Joy is valuable on its own, and it might remind you why you got started in the first place. Consider doing something that feels fun and easy, like going for a walk, bike ride, or fun transit trip. As long as it "isn't nothing," it might give you that spark you need. Courtney Jackson of Ride New Orleans says, "People have a limited amount of capacity to process how everything in the world is constantly terrible all the time. . . . Transit advocates also need to make the work fun."[3] If making your own fun feels like too much effort, join in on the fun that others are making, or ask if someone in your crew might be up for putting on an enjoyable event like a group transit ride. Go outside and try to attune to the transportation-related joy that is around you, such as a group of friends chatting while walking down the sidewalk, a kid learning to ride their bike in the park, or a person seeing their bus pull up to their stop. Joy abounds, and as transportation activists, we are working to make that joy more plentiful. We are on the side of joy.

When tapping into joy doesn't help motivate you, consider tapping into a sense of power. Find your power by asking yourself, "What is something I can do that no one can stop me from doing?" People can't stop you from trying to shift the culture. Making art and telling stories is a powerful way to plant seeds of change. Sometimes people frustrated at the pace of change take things into their own hands. Transportation advocates have made their own benches to put at bus stops and made their own protections for bike lanes with items like plastic posts.[4] Some direct actions yield only temporary results, but they can still help bring groups together and increase people's sense of agency.

Motivated but Tired

When you are motivated but exhausted, rest. Rest in a way that is restful *for you*. Let go of the stereotype of what you think rest *should* be, and "let the soft animal of your body love what it loves," as the poet Mary Oliver reminds us.[5] Carving out the space for rest can be hard, but remember that rest is part of the work. "Effective transportation policy and advocacy require balancing urgency with sustainability—rest and pacing are critical," says transportation justice advocate Haleema Bharoocha.[6] No one is going to make you rest but you, and if you don't rest, your body may break down and force you to do so.

You might just need some time away from advocacy to reconnect with your life outside of it. Ines Sigel of LINK Houston says, "There's so much more to life than just doing the work. Doing other things to help you stay calm and see[ing] that there are other things happening out in the world helps you pause so that you can recharge and keep going."[7] Sigel also explained: "Partnerships and coalition work [are] extremely helpful. . . . If one of our partners has to deal with something else, [the coalition] will still carry the work."[8] If you have a coalition or a team of other volunteer leaders, they can continue the campaign while you take a break.

Unmotivated and Exhausted

You may get to a point where your body, mind, or spirit are so exhausted that it is nearly impossible to be productive. If you stay that way, you may be burned out. Burnout is a level of depletion so profound that basic forms of rest—like a few weeks off advocacy work—provide only a brief respite rather than any sort of long-term recovery. This poses a serious problem to an individual advocate's health, quality of life, and ability to continue their advocacy.

Burnout goes beyond a personal issue; it is a problem for our movement. Overextended activists may be short-tempered or emotionally checked out, which is not a good state to be in when dealing with others. Sometimes burnout can lead to groups disbanding, which effectively eliminates the organizational infrastructure they built. That means new advocates have to start from scratch. Our movement to expand non-car transportation options would be significantly stronger if every group that ever fought for a transit service expansion or street safety improvement had been able to endure to this day.

Avoiding and Healing from Burnout

The way to prevent and treat burnout is by balancing your advocacy, your other stressors, and your joy. Burnout comes from excessively operating outside of our limits, so it's important to stay attuned to what those limits may be. Personally, I consider recovering from burnout like recovering from a serious injury. It can take a while and requires rest. You may be more prone to reinjury, so it's important to ease back into things and remember that other people can help take on the work.

There are lots of great books on the subject of dealing with burnout. Hillary Rettig's *The Lifelong Activist: How to Change the World Without Losing Your Way* is an excellent resource on burnout from the lens of activism. She writes about how doing advocacy over the long term means we need to treat it as part of how we live our lives.

In *Burnout: The Secret to Unlocking the Stress Cycle*, the Nagoski siblings explain, "To be 'well' is not to live in a state of perpetual safety and calm, but to move fluidly from a state of adversity, risk, adventure, or excitement, back to safety and calm, and out again. Stress is not bad for you; being stuck is bad for you."[9] They describe the "stress cycle" as starting from a neutral state, followed by a stressor, followed by a response, and then a resolution. If there isn't a resolution, the stress sticks around. Getting to that resolution can be particularly tricky for advocates since it can take a while to see our dreams come to fruition. Laura Chu Wiens suggests, "You can have the pie in the sky thing you're aiming for, but you also need to be able to identify and celebrate the wins along the way."[10] Get to that resolution by celebrating all of your wins, however small: For example, when it comes to something like a petition, celebrate when you get it out the door, when people sign it, and when you deliver it. It's important to break up advocacy work into more digestible pieces and celebrate our progress. This can help nourish us and help us find more meaning in the work we do.

Managing and completing stress cycles takes knowing your limits, having enough control over your life to take breaks as needed, and having the resources and support to get by. It is easier to do quality work when you are rested, fed, and able to pay all your bills. Transit advocate Lian Chang, who balances her advocacy with her busy life and raising a child, says, "Being involved in activism requires some combination of a supportive partner and/or other adults to take on childcare, flexibility from other organizers when you have a kid in tow, and the good luck of having a kid who's willing and able to go along."[11] You can foster a campaign culture where volunteers form a network of mutual support by providing food, making meetings accessible via remote participation, or offering child-friendly activities so more people can participate. The more supportive you can collectively make your advocacy spaces, the more you will be able to lean on others when you need a break, and vice versa. Being supportive also means honoring people's needs for breaks. Indianapolis City Councilmember Jesse Brown says, "I like to think of it as seasonality rather than burnout. . . . The key is finding ways to keep people involved without expecting the same level of commitment from them all the time."[12]

Ready to Do More, but What?

When you are ready to dive back into campaigning, start with reassessing your situation, as chapter 7 touched on. Experience is one of the best teachers in advocacy, and across each new campaign, you will have learned so much. You might have been too in the thick of things to notice, so take some time to step back and reflect on what you've learned from the experience. Pause, take a breath, and look around. Alone or with your core crew, debrief and ask yourself questions like those shown in box 8.1.

By going through that exercise, you can distill your experiences into concrete lessons learned. In turn, those lessons can inform and strengthen your next organizing effort. For example, you and your team may realize

Box 8.1: Questions for Post-Campaign Reflection

- What have you accomplished?
- What have you learned?
- What worked and what didn't?
- How did things go differently from what you had expected and why might that be?
- What are you better at doing now than you were when you first started?
- How has your understanding shifted about your context?
- In hindsight, how do you think your campaign did?
- Knowing what you know now, what will you do differently next time?

you want to build relationships with groups that weren't even on your radar before, or you may want to win changes in some other arena of decision-making that you have learned to better appreciate. Almost no street safety advocate starts with a campaign to adjust their city's fire code, but they may eventually decide to fight for a fire code that can accommodate street-narrowing interventions. Or transit advocates may find themselves drawn to engage more at their regional Metropolitan Planning Organization than when they first started. When choosing your next campaign, you have several options for next steps.

First, you can fight the next version of the initial fight. No matter how your initial campaign ended, something is probably supposed to happen next. In the event that you won your initial fight, phase two could be a push to speed up implementation or otherwise ensure that nothing goes sideways to ruin your victory. Charting out the official process and the expected timeline will help you see the hurdles that may hobble your victory even at this late stage. Similarly, if you lost your initial fight, there is always an opportunity to take another bite of the apple because our transportation system is always changing. You might not win your budget fight this year, but the budget will be set again next year. You can always keep fighting, and if you want to, you can relitigate past fights, especially if you've built more power than you had when you last tried. Before you decide to revive your fight, check with your team and with your coalition partners to see if they are interested in going another round.

Second, you can run your last campaign's playbook again in a new jurisdiction. Once LINK Houston helped the Gulfton community win a bus route, the group worked with a northeast Houston community to win another one.[13] After the group All Aboard Minnesota helped win the new Borealis Amtrak service from St. Paul to Minneapolis, they pushed to expand service to Fargo, North Dakota.[14] Same core demand, new jurisdiction. In these situations, remember to alter your strategy to match your new context. Incorporate the lessons learned from your last campaign so that you're running an improved version of the playbook.

Third, you can build on your original fight with a complementary effort. You can generate ideas by considering your original issue from a new angle. For example, if your last campaign was a budget fight, you could switch to a policy fight. Or if you lose an effort to prevent fare hikes, you could launch an effort for a low-income transit pass program. Maybe you won but you want to make your fight easier for the next time. For example, as mentioned earlier, after a tumultuous effort to electrify a particular rail corridor, Californians for Electric Rail fought successfully for a law that streamlined the approval process for electrifying rail service. If your initial campaign lost, winning a follow-up campaign like this can shift the political terrain so that your next attempt has fewer hurdles.

Lastly, you can apply your newly developed expertise to different situations. Through your first campaign, you and your group will have built some specialized skills. For example, you may have ended up getting pretty good at navigating the intricacies of the relationships between your state's Department of Transportation (DOT) and your local government. That skill set is something you can use to help advocates in other communities who are gearing up for a campaign regarding the DOT and their local government. Having gone through the process at least once before, you can be a sort of Mary Poppins who comes in, helps out activists who need support in that specialized area, and then leaves to go help the next community or group.

Transportation Advocacy Beyond Campaigning

Taking a step back from a single campaign helps give us a wider perspective. Individual campaigns are like mushroom caps; they are the visible outcropping of a vast mycelium network of ideas, energy, and connections that make up political movements. Throughout my interviews with transportation advocates around the country, there was a consistent theme about how campaigns are just one facet of advocacy. Organizing for transportation change can go far beyond whichever campaigns you are working on at the moment. It can also include community building, providing services, educating community members about how to ride transit or bikes, hosting social rides or other fun events, putting out research reports, and more. Whether or not you have a particular campaign going on, it is still worthwhile to build relationships with local reporters, decision-makers, and allies.

We have so many ways to make change, so much that we need to change, and so much urgency for change. As transportation advocates pushing against entrenched car domination, we are up against a lot. I know firsthand how disheartening and depressing that can feel. Right now, our streets are deadly, our communities are hard to get around, and our climate is being knocked out of whack. Taking on all of that can feel overwhelming. It can feel like too much for any one person, group, or coalition—and that's because it is. But you are not alone.

Changing America's transportation system to center people rather than cars is the work of an overall movement, and you are part of that movement—no matter how small or local your focus is. Your advocacy connects you to a vast web of people trying to do good in this world. Thank you for being part of this movement; I'm glad to have you with us. I plan on continuing to help transportation advocates for at least another few decades, so feel free to reach out!

Even if you picked up this book so you can win a stop sign, and afterward decide to never advocate for anything else again, you are still a part of the movement. You will have made your corner of the world that much better and put future advocates in a stronger position. Your actions will reverberate in ways you will never know.

As mentioned in the introduction, when you win a transportation change, everyone else gets to benefit from it. Our transportation system is something we all share, and our campaigns are also connected. We can learn from each other's experiences and accomplishments. We can win big changes that make our transportation system work better for everyone, including by channeling the organizing that we do in our communities into pushing our federal representatives for nationwide change.

At the root of it all, transportation advocacy is about making the world a better place for everyone. Working to improve the lives of people who you may never know is an act of love, and transportation activism involves love for what the future could be if only things were different. Tapping into that feeling comforts me when times are tough, and I hope it can help you too. I believe that for advocacy to be healthy and sustainable, it needs to connect to the root of all advocacy: love and hope for something better. The work of the advocate is to use our love and passion to make change happen, while helping others do the same.

It takes a lot of work to make our dreams reality, but our dreams are worth fighting for. Transportation advocates fight for the freedom to safely cross the street or easily get where we want to go without endangering our neighbors and destroying the planet. This can be a struggle, but you can also find joy in it. It's fun to build community, and there is pleasure in making friends and allies. There is joy in feeling empowered and having a sense of purpose or being part of something greater than yourself. Seeing your efforts make a difference can also fill you with immense pride. I still beam every time I see seniors and children cross at an intersection I helped make safer. Transportation advocacy is filled with these sorts of life-affirming experiences.

Your desire to make the world safer and more accessible is a noble one. I want you to win the changes that you want, and this book is me betting on you. Even if you lose the occasional campaign, what you build and the work you do brings the world closer to those ideals. You may face opposition, but the main thing you are up against is inertia. The world is as it is until we all change it. So, let's change it! Build power and fight strategically, and you will make a difference. Your transportation dreams are all possible, so now the only question is: Are you ready to fight for them?

Action Points

1) Dream up a change you want for the world.
2) Build community around that shared dream.
3) Fight like hell for it.
4) Rejoice, rest, reengage.
5) Teach others what you learned.

Acknowledgments

Mara, I'm grateful that we are partners in life, activism, adventure, and rest. Thank you for your excellent and thorough editing to make this book significantly more accessible. This book, and my life, are far better because of you.

I also want to give thanks to:

Avery Barrett, my friend and board game business partner at Serious Mischief, for your compassionate and insightful edits, for modeling that feedback is a gift, and for being a deeply thinky/feely/actiony/fighty/playful person. I'm so glad we get to do all of those things together! (Readers, keep an eye out for our forthcoming board game about activism!)

The Island Press team and especially Annie Byrnes, who helped me understand how special book writing is, for your patience as I learned how to code switch from activism-speak to book-speak, and for helping boil this book down so it could really shine. Your invitation to write this book changed my life and hopefully will help lots of people make lots of good changes.

All my friends who were with me in the chaos and creation of this book; my anchor besties Elle and Amanda for consistently cheering me on and reminding me that I am more than my activism. Thank you for your wisdom on the variety of ways to make change and be in this world. And to Brandon, Nicky, Henry, Carissa, Urvi, and Heather. To Mari for being the first person to seriously suggest that a book was something I could write, though the book in question was drastically different than this one (but probably less different than we might think). And to Tommaso for his enthusiasm and support for this project at a pivotal time in the writing process when I really needed it.

My family for their love and especially to my dad Carl for his edits and opinions, and for instilling in me at a young age that traffic violence is entirely preventable. My mother Lauren for her excellence and enthusiasm when it comes to storytelling and moral clarity. Thank you for modeling how to weave and fight for a life of joy and openheartedness. My siblings Austin, Seth, and Celeste for being slightly better than I am at a thing or two and challenging me to keep up; and their spouses Beth, Kate, and Eliana for choosing us and bringing up the average. My niblings Moses, Miles, Amelia, and Max, who are already experts in getting grown-ups to do what they want. Activism takes the same general principles, though it is a bit more complicated.

My extended family for their love and for working to make the world a better place in their own ways. Especially to my most relentless cheerleaders, Aunt Jane and Aunt Maud, leaders in their respective fields, who have consistently encouraged me and helped teach me that what I have to say matters. And to Randi, Sara, Teo, and Eden—without whom I would not have ended up in Oakland!

Grandma Audrey, for her edits, wit, and masterful leadership of the loose coalition that is our big raucous family.

The large umbrella of family on my spouse's side, and in particular my mother-in-law Victoria for helping me veer away from burnout at a critical juncture, for her wisdom on rest, and for her helpful edits to this book; as well as Justin and Katherine for showing that travel for pleasure and doing the work can coincide. And my brother-in-law Brendan, thank you for being a thoughtful sounding board for all sorts of ideas around potential political stunts.

The crews at Traffic Violence Rapid Response, Transbay Coalition, San Francisco Bay Area Bench Collective, and the East Bay Transit Riders Union for all your passion and action to make our corner of the world a better place for all. I'm honored to be figuring out all this stuff together with you. To my frequent coalition partners at Seamless Bay Area, Voices for Public Transportation, Move LA, SPUR, ClimatePlan, Bike East Bay, and Safe Roads Save Lives Coalition, it's an honor to be in the struggle with you.

Special shout-out to Adina Levin for always being a champion of deeper organizing in the transportation space. Thank you for blazing the trail and always being so strategic about it.

East Bay Coffee Ride crew for embodying bike joy.

Sky Croeser and Pam Harris for helping me understand broader contexts of the world, especially at times when my understanding of politics was drastically expanding, and for giving me a range of political frameworks that helped me nurture my values into beliefs.

The people of the distributed solar and storage industry, which I first joined as a teen filled with dreams and a desire to do some good. You are a rowdy bunch of revolutionaries, idealists, ruthless pragmatists, and problem-solvers, and the world is far better for it. I could not have asked for a better proving ground and a more dynamic group of people to be comrade in arms with as I went from being a kid to the political organizer I am today. Thank you for bringing me to California.

My fellow transportation activists around the world, including all those who shared their wisdom and stories with me for this book, whether or not their quotes and anecdotes made it in. This book simply scratches the surface of what your great work entails; I hope this brings in a lot more leaders so y'all can get a little bit of rest.

You, the reader, for trying to do good in the world. I hope that this book is a helpful resource as you seek to do it better.

Everyone who has ever asked or allowed me to explain something, held space for me to attempt it, and helped me improve.

Special thanks to the Refreshments and Resistance crew for holding the space years ago where I could try explaining my "eight elements of political power" theory, which ended up being the foundation of this book and much of my work.

Big thanks to the Streetsblog team, especially Kea, Roger, Melanie, Damien, and Jeff for welcoming me so deeply into the wider world of transportation advocacy.

All the other movements I have been fortunate to be part of. Your values, accomplishments, and collective experiences have made the world better and taught me so much. Especially to movement leaders Jay Carmona, Cayden Mak, Nicole Deane, and Farah Mahesri, who inspire me and helped me understand organizing at a deeper level.

The people and organizations who at times have been my well-funded opposition. Thank you for teaching me that money isn't everything (but it does help a lot), and for the consistent reminder that being right is one thing; winning is another.

The politicians who have been enthusiastic inside-game allies while inspiring and challenging me to treat government as the powerful tool for good that it can be, from city councilmembers to transit agency directors to state legislators.

The people who want to tear it all down, the people who want to reform our deeply problematic system, and the people who want to build new better institutions at levels from the interpersonal to the international: You are all right, you have more in common than you might care to admit, and we will only win together.

The authors and explainers, for explicitly teaching me so much and for teaching me through their example so much about teaching others: Rebecca Solnit, Jane McAlevey, Becky Bond, Zack Exley, adrienne maree brown, bell hooks, Jessica Valenti, Brené Brown, Helen Zaltzman, Eric Molinsky, Avery Trufelman, Overly Sarcastic Productions, and *Extra History*.

The artists who create complicated worlds and hold a mirror up to our own, you inspire me, nourish my soul, and as Toni Cade Bambara said, "make the revolution irresistible": Becky Chambers, Rebecca Sugar, Caro De Robertis, Octavia Butler, Garth Nix (whose depiction of working magic is, to me, the closest description of what writing this book felt like), Ruthanna Emrys, the team behind the *Dungeons and Daddies* podcast, the creators of *Newsies*, Emily Henry, R. K. Milholland, Zach Weinersmith, and Jeph Jacques.

Finally, the people whose work has enabled me to do this work, from farmworkers to transit workers and everyone in between. Without you, this book—and whatever advocacy it sparks—would not exist.

Notes

Introduction

1. *Merriam-Webster Dictionary*, "politics," accessed November 21, 2024, https://www.merriam-webster.com/dictionary/politics.
2. "Highway and Road Expenditures," Urban Institute, accessed November 21, 2024, https://www.urban.org/policy-centers/cross-center-initiatives/state-and-local-finance-initiative/state-and-local-backgrounders/highway-and-road-expenditures.
3. People for Bikes, *U.S. Bicycling Participation Study: Report of Findings from the 2018 Survey* (Corona Insights, 2019), https://wsd-pfb-sparkinfluence.s3.amazonaws.com/uploads/2019/03/Corona-Report-for-PFB-Participation-2018-for-Website.pdf.
4. "Public Transportation Facts," American Public Transportation Association, https://www.apta.com/news-publications/public-transportation-facts.
5. Office of Highway Policy Information, "Highway Statistics 2020," US Department of Transportation, modified September 24, 2022, https://www.fhwa.dot.gov/policyinformation/statistics/2020.
6. Nico Savidge, "How Did the Hopkins Street Bike Lane Project Turn Into a 'Culture War'?" Berkeleyside, February 23, 2023, https://www.berkeleyside.org/2023/02/23/hopkins-bike-lane-project-north-berkeley.
7. Anna Zivarts, in discussion with the author, November 2024.
8. Laura Chu Wiens, in discussion with the author, February 2024.
9. "Celebrating Labor Organizer César Chávez: Talk to One Person, Then

Another, and Another," Corporate Accountability, March 31, 2018, https://corporateaccountability.org/blog/celebrating-labor-organizer-cesar-chavez-talk-to-one-person-then-another-and-another.

10. Jeff Guo, "We Counted Literally Every Road in America. Here's What We Learned," *The Washington Post*, March 6, 2023, https://www.washingtonpost.com/blogs/govbeat/wp/2015/03/06/these-are-the-most-popular-street-names-in-every-state.
11. Amy Smaldone and Mark L. J. Wright, "Local Governments in the U.S.: A Breakdown by Number and Type," Federal Reserve Bank of St. Louis, March 14, 2024, https://www.stlouisfed.org/publications/regional-economist/2024/march/local-governments-us-number-type.
12. Rebecca Solnit, *Hope in the Dark: Untold Histories, Wild Possibilities* (Haymarket Books, 2019).
13. "American States Are Bailing Out Public Transport," *The Economist*, June 15, 2023, https://www.economist.com/united-states/2023/06/15/american-states-are-bailing-out-public-transport.
14. Michael Wojcik, in discussion with the author, March 2024.

Chapter 1: Politics Isn't a Dirty Word

1. Bakari Height, in discussion with the author, February 2024.
2. Mario Moretto, "Maine Governor Vetoes Every Democratic Bill Out of Spite," *Governing*, June 9, 2015, https://www.governing.com/archive/tns-lepage-veto-threat.html; Jim Tassé, discussion with the author, April 2024.
3. Tassé, discussion.
4. Donald C. Shoup, *The High Cost of Free Parking* (Planners Press, 2011).
5. "National Household Travel Survey Daily Travel Quick Facts," Bureau of Transportation Statistics, May 31, 2017, https://www.bts.gov/statistical-products/surveys/national-household-travel-survey-daily-travel-quick-facts.
6. United States Census Bureau, "New Census Report Shows Public Transportation Commuters Concentrated in Large Metro Areas of the United States," April 1, 2021, https://www.census.gov/newsroom/press-releases/2021/public-transportation-commuters.html.
7. "State: Rates of Biking and Walking," Benchmarking Report by the League of American Bicyclists, March 8, 2024, https://data.bikeleague.org/data/states-rates-of-active-commuting.
8. Kalli Krumpos, discussion with the author, May 2024.
9. Krumpos, discussion.
10. Naomi Klein, *This Changes Everything: Capitalism vs. The Climate* (Simon and Schuster, 2014).

11. Ryan Gravel, *Where We Want to Live: Reclaiming Infrastructure for a New Generation of Cities* (St. Martin's Publishing Group, 2016).
12. URS Corporation, Connectics Transportation Group, DW & Associates, PBS&J, Planners for Environmental Quality, and Sycamore Consulting, Review of Detailed Screening Results and Selection of Locally Preferred Alternative, accessed May 25, 2025.
13. Patrick Quinn, "Atlanta Mayor Sheds Light on Timeline, Funding for 4 New MARTA Rail Stations | One-on-One Interview," Atlanta News First, April 16, 2024, https://www.atlantanewsfirst.com/2024/04/16/atlanta-mayor-sheds-light-timeline-funding-4-new-marta-rail-stations-one-on-one-interview.
14. Quinn, "Atlanta Mayor Sheds Light."
15. Josh of Radical Planning, discussion with the author, October 2024.
16. Josh of Radical Planning, discussion.
17. Josh of Radical Planning, discussion.
18. Josh of Radical Planning, discussion.
19. Eric Rogers, discussion with the author, April 2024.
20. Friends of Ocean Beach Park (@GreatHwyPark), "Unfortunately, today's 4pm Q&A for families at South Sunset Playground had to be cancelled. Prop K opponents showed up with a bullhorn and were harassing attendees. This isn't something we want to put families through. Stay tuned for a future events to learn more about Prop K." X, October 3, 2024, 4:16 p.m., https://x.com/GreatHwyPark/status/1841980789032157267.

Chapter 2: Picking Your Battles and Outlining Your Campaign

1. Ines Sigel, discussion with the author, October 2024.
2. LINK Houston, accessed November 22, 2024, https://linkhouston.org; Sigel, discussion.
3. Michael Wojcik, discussion with the author, May 2024.
4. Abbey Seitz, discussion with the author, October 2024.
5. Megan Ramey, discussion with the author, November 2024
6. Ramey, discussion.
7. Jordi Honey-Rosés, "Lessons from the Bike Bus Summit," April 3, 2023, https://citylabbcn.org/lessons-from-the-bike-bus-summit.
8. "Drunk Driving Fatality Statistics," Foundation for Advancing Alcohol Responsibility, https://www.responsibility.org/alcohol-statistics/drunk-driving-statistics/drunk-driving-fatality-statistics.
9. "Join the 'I Bike, I Buy Stuff' Campaign," Washington Area Bicyclist Association, https://waba.org/action-page/join-the-i-bike-i-buy-stuff-campaign.

10. Kalli Krumpos, discussion with the author, May 2024.
11. Jesse Brown, discussion with the author, November 2024.
12. Beth Osborne, discussion with the author, October 2024.
13. David Simmons, discussion with the author, May 2024.
14. Simmons, discussion.
15. Calelectric, "How Environmental Law Holds Back Cleaner and Better Rail | Part 2: Atherton vs. Caltrain Electrification," Californians for Electric Rail, April 3, 2024, https://calelectricrail.org/how-environmental-law-holds-back-cleaner-better-rail-part-2-atherton-vs-caltrain-electrification.
16. Todd Scott, discussion with the author, April 2024.
17. Laura Chu Wiens, discussion with the author, February 2024.
18. Robert Smith, "When U.S. Paid Off the Entire National Debt (and Why It Didn't Last)," NPR, April 15, 2011, https://www.npr.org/sections/money/2011/04/15/135423586/when-the-u-s-paid-off-the-entire-national-debt-and-why-it-didnt-last.
19. "What Are the Sources of Revenue for State and Local Governments?," Tax Policy Center, accessed November 22, 2024, https://www.taxpolicycenter.org/briefing-book/what-are-sources-revenue-state-and-local-governments.
20. Rob Hull, "Speed Bumps Turn 40! Rob Hull Asks: Are the Traffic-Slowing Measures Still Fit for Purpose?," This Is Money, October 8, 2023, https://www.thisismoney.co.uk/money/cars/article-12598819/Speed-bumps-Britain-roads-40-years.html.
21. "NHTSA Estimates for 2022 Show Roadway Fatalities Remain Flat After Two Years of Dramatic Increases," National Highway Traffic Safety Administration, April 20, 2023, https://www.nhtsa.gov/press-releases/traffic-crash-death-estimates-2022; "Number of Reported Murder and Nonnegligent Manslaughter Cases in the United States from 1990 to 2023," Statista, November 12, 2024, https://www.statista.com/statistics/191134/reported-murder-and-nonnegligent-manslaughter-cases-in-the-us-since-1990.
22. "Safe Streets and Roads for All (SS4A) Grant Program," US Department of Transportation, 2024, https://www.transportation.gov/grants/SS4A; Tara O'Neill Hayes, "The Economic Costs of the U.S. Criminal Justice System," American Action Forum, July 16, 2020, https://www.americanactionforum.org/research/the-economic-costs-of-the-u-s-criminal-justice-system.
23. "Transportation of Texas Funding for Years 2024–2025," Texas Depart-

ment of Transportation FTP Server, 2023, https://ftp.txdot.gov/pub/txdot-info/fin/funding-brochure.pdf.

24. Kelsey Huse, discussion with the author, October 2024.
25. Irene Fernando, discussion with the author, May 2024.

Chapter 3: Understanding Your Context and Making Connections

1. Deb Banks, discussion with the author, April 2024.
2. Andrew Boyd, "Power Mapping," Beautiful Trouble, https://beautifultrouble.org/toolbox/tool/power-mapping.
3. Michael Wojcik, discussion with the author, May 2024.
4. Wojcik, discussion.
5. Romic Aevaz, "Eno Releases Major Report on U.S. Transit Costs and Project Delivery," Eno Center for Transportation, July 30, 2021, https://enotrans.org/article/eno-releases-major-report-on-u-s-transit-costs-and-project-delivery.
6. Yaohui Zhang and Shitong Chen, "Original Design of the SSJ900-Type Bridge Girder Erection Machine," ASCE Library, April 26, 2012, https://ascelibrary.org/doi/10.1061/41039%28345%29285.
7. Zachary B. Wolf, "4 Years, 1.2 Million Lives and Trillions of Dollars Later, a Rematch," CNN, March 13, 2024, https://www.cnn.com/2024/03/13/politics/covid-anniversary-what-matters/index.html.
8. Reis Thebault and Alice Li, "Pandemic: Three Years In: Inside the Movement to Remake America's City Streets," *The Washington Post*, March 13, 2023, https://www.washingtonpost.com/nation/interactive/2023/pedestrian-safety-covid-pandemic.
9. Kaleah Mcilwain, "Crews Complete Demolition of I-95 Collapse Site and Begin Rebuilding Phase," NBC Philadelphia, June 15, 2023, https://www.nbcphiladelphia.com/news/local/i-95-reconstruction-watch-live-as-the-bridge-is-being-rebuilt/3586370.
10. David Simmons, discussion with the author, May 2024.
11. "World Naked Bike Ride San Francisco: All You Need to Know," KQED, April 8, 2024, https://www.kqed.org/arts/13955410/world-naked-bike-ride-2024-where-to-meet-420-dress-code.
12. Hannah Pinski, "Metro Transit: Extended Light-Rail Service for Taylor Swift's Eras Tour Was a Success," *The Minnesota Star Tribune*, June 29, 2023, https://www.startribune.com/metro-transit-extended-light-rail-service-for-taylor-swifts-eras-tour-was-a-success/600286317.
13. Irene Fernando, discussion with the author, May 2024.

14. Fernando, discussion.
15. Todd Scott, discussion with the author, April 2024.
16. Scott, discussion.
17. US Department of Justice Civil Rights Division, *Investigation of the Ferguson Police Department* (Department of Justice, March 4, 2015), https://www.justice.gov/sites/default/files/opa/press-releases/attachments/2015/03/04/ferguson_police_department_report_1.pdf.
18. US DOJ, *Investigation of the Ferguson Police Department*; "Fatal Car Crashes and Road Traffic Accidents in Ferguson, Missouri," City-Data, https://www.city-data.com/accidents/acc-Ferguson-Missouri.html.
19. US DOJ, *Investigation of the Ferguson Police Department.*
20. Rachel Clarke and Mariano Castillo, "Michael Brown Shooting: What Darren Wilson Told the Ferguson Grand Jury," CNN, November 26, 2014, https://edition.cnn.com/2014/11/25/justice/ferguson-grand-jury-documents.
21. Thomas Gibbons and Post Staff, "Military Veterans See Deeply Flawed Police Response in Ferguson," *The Washington Post*, August 14, 2014, https://www.washingtonpost.com/news/checkpoint/wp/2014/08/14/military-veterans-see-deeply-flawed-police-response-in-ferguson; "Ferguson Shooting: Protests Spread Across US," BBC, November 26, 2014, https://www.bbc.com/news/world-us-canada-30203526.
22. "Police-Public Contact Survey (PPCS)," Bureau of Justice Statistics, https://bjs.ojp.gov/data-collection/police-public-contact-survey-ppcs#publications-0; "2024 Police Violence Report," Mapping Police Violence, https://policeviolencereport.org.
23. Carter Lavin, "Bike Lanes vs. the Carceral State," *Convergence Magazine*, December 15, 2023, https://convergencemag.com/articles/bike-lanes-vs-the-carceral-state.
24. "Cárdenas First Bill Honors Cesár Estrada Chavéz," Office of Congressman Tony Cárdenas, 2013, https://cardenas.house.gov/media-center/press-releases/c-rdenas-first-bill-honors-ces-r-estrada-ch-vez-el-primer-proyecto-de.
25. Bill Nesper, discussion with the author, April 2024.
26. Michael Kelley, discussion with the author, November 2024.
27. Laura Chu Wiens, discussion with the author, February 2024.
28. José Antonio Zayas Cabán, discussion with the author, November 2024.
29. Zayas Cabán, discussion.
30. "Connecting California," HNTB, 2024, https://www.hntb.com/designer/connecting-california.

31. "Alumni Heat Map," Fresno State Alumni Association, https://alumni.fresnostate.edu/about/alumni-heat-map.html.
32. Alec Nolan, "Battle for the Valley: Fresno State Gears Up for 87th Meeting with San Jose State," ABC 30 Action News, October 21, 2024, https://abc30.com/post/battle-valley-fresno-state-gears-87th-meeting-san-jose/15452568.
33. Nesper, discussion.

Chapter 4: You Can't Win Alone, So Build Out a Team

1. Michael Kelley, discussion with the author, November 2024.
2. Irene Fernando, discussion with the author, May 2024.
3. Ines Sigel, discussion with the author, October 2024.
4. Kalli Krumpos, discussion with the author, May 2024.
5. Krumpos, discussion.
6. Deb Banks, discussion with the author, April 2024.
7. Bakari Height, discussion with the author, February 2024.
8. Laura Chu Wiens, discussion with the author, February 2024.
9. Abbey Seitz, discussion with the author, October 2024.
10. Jesse Brown, discussion with the author, November 2024.
11. Chu Wiens, discussion.
12. Starhawk, *The Empowerment Manual: A Guide for Collaborative Groups* (New Society Publishers, 2011).
13. Patricia Raub, discussion with the author, March 2024.
14. Amy Glidden, discussion with the author, March 2024.
15. Glidden, discussion.
16. Starhawk, *The Empowerment Manual.*
17. Glidden, discussion.
18. Starhawk, *The Empowerment Manual.*
19. tamika l. butler, "Last Year, The Bike Industry Promised Inclusivity. But Advocacy Allies Still Don't Get It," *Bicycling*, July 1, 2021, https://www.bicycling.com/culture/a36688353/bike-industry-inclusive-safety.
20. Transbay Coalition, https://www.transbaycoalition.org.
21. Courtney Jackson, discussion with the author, March 2024.

Chapter 5: Win Bigger in Coalition

1. Eric Rogers, discussion with the author, April 2024.
2. Rogers, discussion.
3. *Merriam-Webster Dictionary*, "coalition," accessed November 23, 2024, https://www.merriam-webster.com/dictionary/coalition.

4. FastCo Works, "Shaping the Future of Aging," Fast Company, September 1, 2020, https://www.fastcompany.com/90532973/shaping-the-future-of-aging.
5. Luke Hoffman, discussion with the author, April 2024.
6. Mike Ege, "'Not Optional': Newsom Faces Pushback Over Transit, Climate Cuts," *The San Francisco Standard*, January 11, 2023, https://sfstandard.com/2023/01/11/not-optional-newsom-faces-pushback-over-transit-climate-cuts.
7. Daniel Villaseñor, "Nearly $2 Billion Going to California Public Transit," Governor of California, July 8, 2024, https://www.gov.ca.gov/2024/07/08/nearly-2-billion-going-to-california-public-transit.
8. Abbey Seitz, discussion with the author, October 2024.
9. Seitz, discussion.
10. Anna Zivarts, discussion with the author, November 2024.
11. Zivarts, discussion.
12. Haleema Bharoocha, discussion with the author, November 2024.
13. Bharoocha, discussion.
14. "Not One More Girl Phase I," Bay Area Rapid Transit, https://www.bart.gov/guide/safety/gbv/campaign.
15. Deb Banks, discussion with the author, April 2024.
16. Courtney Jackson, discussion with the author, March 2024.
17. Megan Ramey, discussion with the author, November 2024.
18. Beth Osborne, discussion with the author, October 2024.
19. Bakari Height, discussion with the author, February 2024.
20. Michael Wojcik, discussion with the author, May 2024.
21. Wojcik, discussion.
22. Laura Chu Wiens, discussion with the author, February 2024.
23. Jackson, discussion.
24. SacMoves Coalition, https://sacmoves.org.
25. Banks, discussion.
26. Chu Wiens, discussion.
27. Chu Wiens, discussion.
28. "Positionality," NYU Reads, https://guides.nyu.edu/nyu-reads/how-the-word-is-passed/positionality.

Chapter 6: Deploying an Inside/Outside Strategy

1. Bill Nesper, discussion with the author, April 2024.
2. Nesper, discussion.
3. Beth Osborne, discussion with the author, October 2024.

4. Osborne, discussion.
5. Osborne, discussion.
6. Nicholas Mazzoni, "Burlingame Block Party Over," *San Mateo Daily Journal*, August 25, 2023, https://www.smdailyjournal.com/news/local/burlingame-block-party-over/article_bbea6e86-42fa-11ee-be4d-23ddd0642788.html.
7. Mazzoni, "Burlingame Block Party Over."
8. David Simmons, discussion with the author, May 2024.
9. *Steven Universe: The Movie*, directed by Rebecca Sugar (Cartoon Network Studios, 2019), 1 hr., 22 min.
10. Michael Kelley, discussion with the author, November 2024.
11. Kelley, discussion.
12. Steve Grammer, discussion with the author, March 2024.
13. Grammer, discussion.
14. Nesper, discussion.
15. Josh of Radical Planning, discussion with the author, October 2024.
16. Nesper, discussion.

Chapter 7: Deploying Tactics to Win

1. Luke Hoffman, discussion with the author, April 2024.
2. "ABQ RIDE Zero Fares," City of Albuquerque, 2024, https://www.cabq.gov/transit/how-to-ride/zero-fares.
3. Izzy Goodman, "Canvassing in Times Like These," Better Outcomes Consulting, https://www.betteroutcomesconsulting.org/blog/canvassing-in-times-ike-these.
4. Seth Bush, discussion with the author, September 2024.
5. José Antonio Zayas Cabán, discussion with the author, November 2024.
6. Beth Osborne, discussion with the author, October 2024.
7. Osborne, discussion.
8. Gersh Kuntzman, "Monday's Headlines: Protest Season Begins Edition," *Streetsblog NYC*, June 10, 2024, https://nyc.streetsblog.org/2024/06/10/mondays-headlines-protest-season-begins-edition; Rachel Dobkin, "New York Governor Launches Revised Congestion Pricing System," *Newsweek*, November 14, 2024, https://www.newsweek.com/new-york-congestion-pricing-kathy-hochul-1986105.
9. Lian Chang, discussion with the author, November 2024.
10. Jesse Brown, discussion with the author, November 2024.
11. Michael Wojcik, discussion with the author, May 2024.
12. Ines Sigel, discussion with the author, October 2024.

Conclusion

1. Irene Fernando, discussion with the author, May 2024.
2. Emily Nagoski and Amelia Nagoski, *Burnout: The Secret to Unlocking the Stress Cycle* (Random House, 2019).
3. Courtney Jackson, discussion with the author, March 2024.
4. SFBA Bench Collective, 2025, https://sfbabc.org; Ysabelle Kempe, "Guerrilla Urbanists Are 'Doing It Our Damn Selves,'" Smart Cities Dive, May 23, 2024, https://www.smartcitiesdive.com/news/guerrilla-urbanists-crosswalks-bus-stop-benches/716773.
5. Mary Oliver, "Wild Geese," in *Dream Work* (The Atlantic Monthly Press, 1986).
6. Haleema Bharoocha, discussion with the author, November 2024.
7. Ines Sigel, discussion with the author, October 2024.
8. Sigel, discussion.
9. Nagoski and Nagoski, *Burnout.*
10. Laura Chu Wiens, discussion with the author, February 2024.
11. Lian Chang, discussion with the author, November 2024.
12. Jesse Brown, discussion with the author, November 2024.
13. Sigel, discussion.
14. Brian Nelson, discussion with the author, November 2024.

About the Author

Credit: Heather Hryciw

Carter Lavin is a climate and transportation activist based in Oakland, California, who helps organizations and individuals across North America hone their strategy and build political power. Carter has directly supported and trained nonprofits, candidates, grassroots groups, businesses, and hundreds of individuals to win on the issues that matter to them at the local, regional, and state levels. He is a cofounder of the transportation advocacy group Transbay Coalition and the board game design company Serious Mischief. To learn more and see how he can help your efforts, visit www.CarterLavin.com.